BITTERSWEET

Noma Bar

Foreword by Michael Bierut
With 445 illustrations, 400 in colour

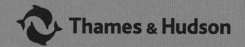
Thames & Hudson

FOREWORD

Foreword

Noma Bar is a magician. He turns cats into dogs, sheep into wolves, tulips into tables, and sandals into sunbathers. And as with any great magician, the trick is so deft and effortless you can barely trust the evidence of your own eyes.

He realized early the power of communicating through images. Arriving in London straight from design school in Jerusalem, he found himself looking for work in a culture where the alphabet was completely different, where people read in the opposite direction, and where books began at the front instead of the back. He was forced, as too few of us are, to go back to basics. He was forced to rediscover that principle so well articulated by John Berger: 'Seeing comes before words. The child looks and recognizes before it can speak.'

Describing his own process, designer Alan Fletcher, a hero of Bar's, once said, 'You don't really see something unless you draw it, or at least until you mentally draw it. It makes you look at things.' Noma Bar's drawings are deceptively simple. Flat colours, minimal detail, nothing more than necessary. But when we look at his drawings, we see exactly what he intends us to see.

One of his simplest drawings is a plump white rectangle, its two ends suggesting faces in profile (pages 170–71). It delivers its meaning with immediacy and concision: *Pillow Talk*. Looking at it, like so much of the work in this book, raises not one but two questions. What is going on in Noma Bar's mind? And what is going on in ours?

The second question is the important one: it goes to the heart of how we perceive the world. The way we convert shapes and colours into coherent meaning has been the subject of much study. In his book *Reductionism in Art and Brain Science*, neuroscientist Eric Kandel describes the complex process by which we reconcile sensation and perception. Abstraction, he writes, 'requires the beholder to substitute primary process thinking – the language of the unconscious, which easily forms connections between different objects and ideas and has no need of time or space – for secondary process thinking, the language of the conscious ego, which is logical and requires time and space coordinates.' Bar's work succeeds in connecting these two realms.

His series of celebrity portraits is the most vivid demonstration of his mastery; the challenge is not merely to communicate a face, but a very specific face. This requires abstract thinking, but not abstract form. Consider his portrait of George W. Bush (page 237), at once completely unmistakable, and – since it is somehow composed entirely from the notorious silhouette of an Abu Ghraib prisoner – utterly devastating. This shock of recognition is repeatedly invoked by Bar's work. Again and again, he finds a place to unite two wildly different visual ideas, and negotiates the meeting with consummate finesse. And he does it apparently without effort.

To perform this feat, as he does on every page of this book, is a remarkable achievement. Magicians make their tricks look easy. So does Noma Bar.

Michael Bierut

LESS

MORE

It was 1997. My girlfriend (now my wife) and I, both students, were hungry for information and knowledge. Escaping to London from our design college in Jerusalem, we went through endless independent bookshops in Charing Cross Road, looking for anything special, authentic or inspirational. After a while we discovered a shop called Zwemmer's, which was heaven for graphic-design specialists like us. We had never before seen a whole shop dedicated to our discipline (in fact, it is still unusual), and we spent the rest of our trip there, reading, looking, sniffing and buying design books.

Through looking at those books I discovered the work of the great Alan Fletcher (1931–2006) – a big inspiration – and of many other British designers and architects. I was looking for books about typography, since I had become interested in Hebrew type design. The internet was in its infancy, and the knowledge was in bookshops like this. We felt Zwemmer's was the sign that London was the right place for us, that there was a scene there, and so we vowed to move to the city as soon as we had graduated.

I soon found that there wasn't a great demand for my Hebrew type portfolio in London. We were living in a small studio flat, with very little money, and earning a living using my main tools – type and language – looked more distant than ever. So I went back to basics, drawing my hands, trying out facial expressions in front of the mirror, spending endless nights drawing my silent language. I looked at street signs, pictograms and iconography and started to use them to tell stories. In an attempt to find a way forward, I made a few postcards and sent them to Alan Fletcher. Two days later I received a letter:

Noma Bar
I thank you for your cards. I like them. I will also post them.
Actually I am not in a context to commission work as I work alone.
Your time would be better spent seeing the Colour Supplements
who should know about you.

Regards
Alan Fletcher

I sent my postcards off and received a great response from *The Guardian*, *Time Out* and other national publications. As I worked on commissions, I made fascinating new visual discoveries and embraced new ideas. I didn't want to spend time on decoration and unnecessary detail that would detract from the image's message, so I made sure always to put

the idea at the forefront, trying for maximum communication with minimal elements. There is a very long way to be travelled between my initial idea or inspiration and a finished work for publication or exhibition, and that in itself is a great discipline.

One thing the human brain is very fond of – and mine is no exception – is to see faces in inanimate objects. My explorations of this with found objects and cast-offs (see opposite) have brought me all kinds of ideas, whether I'm sitting in the woods, looking around me at the natural debris on the ground, or bemoaning the breakdown of my laptop just before a crucial deadline (page 244). This is carried through into illustrations as diverse as *Open Face* (page 19) and my charity ping-pong bat (page 43). The social role of the designer is important to me, and I try always to take jobs with some social benefit.

This chapter is a collection of fifteen years' worth of personal and commissioned work, from screenprints, book jackets and magazine covers to posters and projects for the Victoria and Albert Museum, IBM, Volkswagen, *Chineasy*, the *New York Times*, *The Guardian*, *Wallpaper** and more. For some, such as *Chineasy*, I have been involved in something new and exciting from the start, and helped to shape it; for others, such as the V&A, I have been honoured to contribute to the visual history of something much older than me. I haven't stopped working since my first commission, for *Time Out*, and although it can be difficult to balance professional demands with those of my family, I am constantly inspired and stimulated by the variety of commissions I receive and the ideas they produce.

Look Out, screenprint, 2013

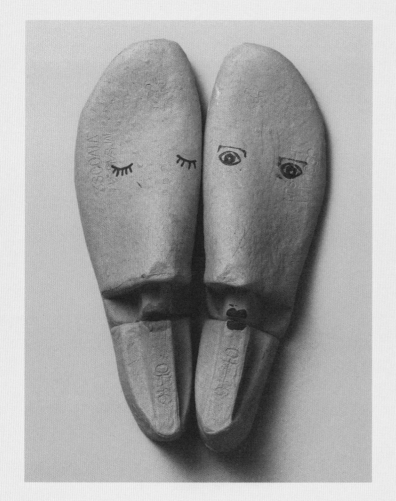

Spin Cycle, wood, metal and paint, 2011

Which Came First?, screenprint, 2013

66 I can be pretty shy. I work long hours, usually alone, and most of the day I'm out and about with my pencil and sketchbook. But often I'm asked to give talks about my life and work, and then a hidden survival instinct surfaces and I find myself chatting about even my personal life to 1,000 strangers. It's a liberating experience, and I call it 'winter shower': you don't want to get in, but when you're in you don't want to get out. **99**

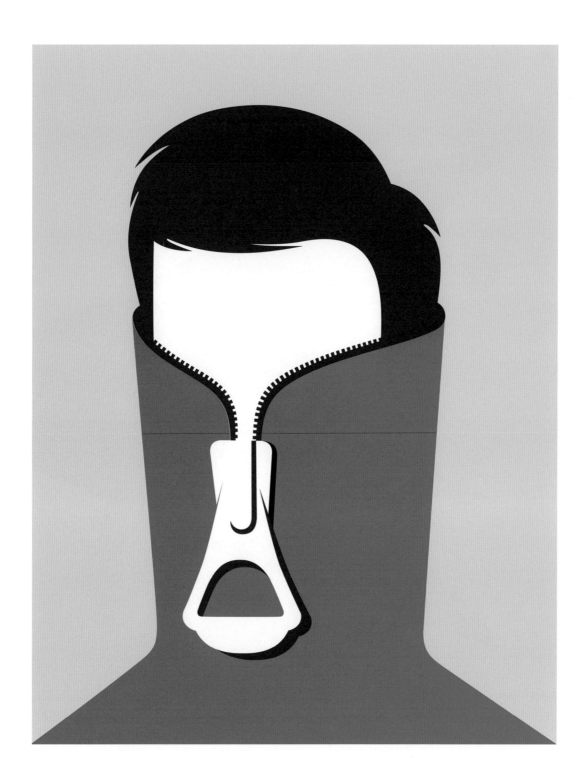

Shy Guy, screenprint, 2009

Therein Lies the Tail, screenprint, 2012

66 I made the sculpture version of this illustration for my exhibition 'Look Out' at L'Imprimerie Gallery, Paris, in 2014. The opening night of the show was great; the gallery looked fabulous and there was plenty of champagne, but suddenly an explosion rang out. Everyone looked towards the centre of the gallery to see the sculpture lying smashed on the floor, punched by a drunken magazine editor who thought the balloon was an interactive art piece. I'm working on the next edition of *Pop Art* – this one will be contained in a Perspex box. **99**

Pop Art, metal, fibreglass and wood, 2014

Pop Art, screenprint, 2012

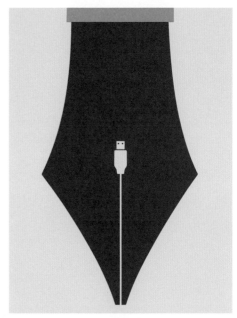

As part of its 'Smarter Planet' campaign, which was launched in 2009, IBM teamed up with Ogilvy Paris and Noma for a set of posters to illustrate what it meant by 'smarter'. The posters showed examples of clever things happening around the world, such as food becoming more traceable and small companies cutting their carbon footprints. The project – Noma's first collaboration with an advertising agency – soon went viral. The posters were picked up across the world, were honoured by D&AD and won numerous accolades including silver and bronze at the London International Awards in 2010, as well as gold and silver at the Cannes Lions International Festival of Creativity and bronze at the New York Festivals International Advertising Awards in 2011.

This page and opposite: Posters for 'Smarter Planet', IBM global campaign, 2009–12

This page and opposite: Posters for 'Smarter Planet', IBM global campaign, 2009–12

66 While I was drawing in Highgate Woods in north London, I witnessed the meeting of two Labradors. The black dog stuck his nose under the raised tail of the white one; after a few seconds he left, but she stayed with her tail up, looking for him. I captured that moment with my pen. The illustration has since been produced as a print, a cut-out and a sculpture. 99

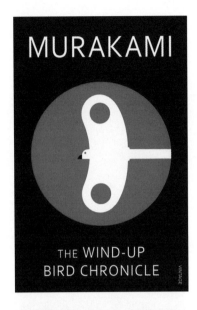

MURAKAMI

THE WIND-UP
BIRD CHRONICLE

VINTAGE

MURAKAMI

SPUTNIK
SWEETHEART

VINTAGE

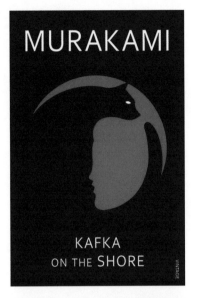

MURAKAMI

KAFKA
ON THE SHORE

VINTAGE

MURAKAMI

NORWEGIAN
WOOD

VINTAGE

MURAKAMI

AFTER DARK

VINTAGE

MURAKAMI

SOUTH OF THE BORDER,
WEST OF THE SUN

VINTAGE

When the publisher Vintage redesigned its Haruki Murakami backlist, it commissioned Noma to produce new covers, which were later made into screenprints. Noma's characteristically ambiguous illustrations, done to a grid prescribed by the publisher, match Murakami's writing, which plays on illusions of reality and hidden ideas. *Creative Review* ran a competition to suggest titles for imaginary Murakami books, and offered a set of the screenprints as first prize.

This page and opposite: Covers for Vintage editions of Haruki Murakami's novels, screenprints, 2012

66 I was coming back to London from Brighton on the train, and there was a man sitting next to the window. He was very drunk and dribbling, and it was all a bit nasty. But suddenly the train stopped by a round neon light, and the scene was transformed into something rather beautiful; it seemed almost as though the moon was all around him, protecting him. I'm always reacting to and documenting things around me, and this is an example of an instant that became a screenprint and a cut-out; it was also given a full page in the 2016 edition of *A Smile in the Mind.* **99**

Vocal Fry, for The Guardian, 24 July 2015

In 2013 Volkswagen commissioned a set of posters for its 'See Film Differently' campaign by DDB UK. The three short films made to accompany the images speculated on the inspiration for famous aspects of these well-known movies.

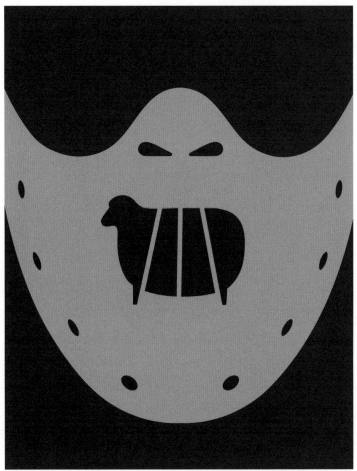

These two three-dimensional pieces were made for Noma's exhibition 'Bitter Sweet' at the KK Outlet gallery in London. Both started life as illustrations for *The Guardian*.

Blind Optimism, wood, metal and paint, 2010

Epic Fail, wood, metal and paint, 2010

This range of stationery was commissioned by *The Guardian* to illustrate playfully the newspaper's various strands. The brief for each section was a single line of text, such as 'Follow the leaders' for the news section and 'Don't be a fashion victim' for the fashion section. The images appeared on the covers of notebooks and diaries, and limited-edition prints were also produced. Shown here are (from left) Fashion, Music and Books & Literature.

Don't Be a Fashion Victim (left) and *Make Some Notes* (right), The Guardian collection, 2012

Double Bill, screenprint, 2013

66 One sunny day in Waterlow Park, north London, sparrows on a branch near the lake and a duck in the water were united by perspective for just a second – enough time for my eye and brain to capture the moment. I drew a graphic interpretation and released it as a screenprint. For most of my life my brain was trained to read and write from right to left, since that is the way Hebrew works. When I moved to London, it took me a while to get used to picking up a book and not checking the back cover first. Over the years, changing the orientation of my reading and writing seems to have affected my sight: my eyes now scan from both sides. **99**

Russian Racquet, for Ace, February 2009

In 2015 Noma designed this hand-painted paddle for Fivefootsix's charity auction 'The Art of Ping Pong', an event for which various artists are invited to design bats. The pieces are then auctioned to raise funds for BBC Children in Need. The Russian doll (opposite) was created for an article about the dominance of Russian players in women's tennis. The two works use the characteristic shape of the bat and racquet in very different ways: one quite simply, to produce a charismatic Pinocchio-like face with an improbable nose; the other to summon the idea of Russia instantly while also playing with the female image. Both pieces contain more references than you will notice at first glance.

The image opposite was made for the group exhibition 'Un homme juste est quand même un homme mort' at the Palais de Tokyo, Paris, in 2013. The theme was 'creativity'. All three illustrations on this spread were produced as screenprints for Eyestorm, the London-based online gallery for contemporary art.

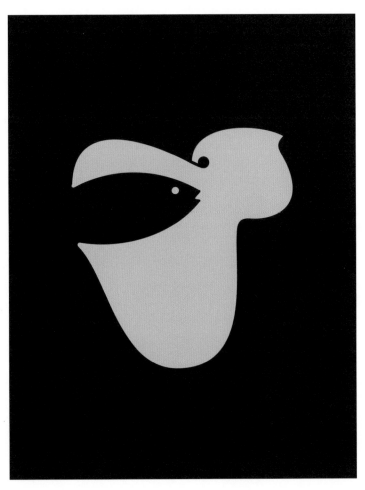

Left: *Look Out*, screenprint, 2013 / Right: *Evolutionary Thought I*, screenprint, 2013

Facing Up, screenprint, 2013

A racing car appears in the negative space of these two iconic helmets facing off in the film *Rush* (2013). Set in the glamorous golden age of Formula 1 racing in the 1970s, the movie dramatizes the true story of the rivalry between the ambitious and brilliant racing drivers James Hunt and Niki Lauda.

New York served as the graphic background for these two illustrations based on the film *The Wolf of Wall Street* (2013) and the long-running television series *Mad Men* (2007–15).

The Wolf of Wall Street, for Empire Review, June 2014

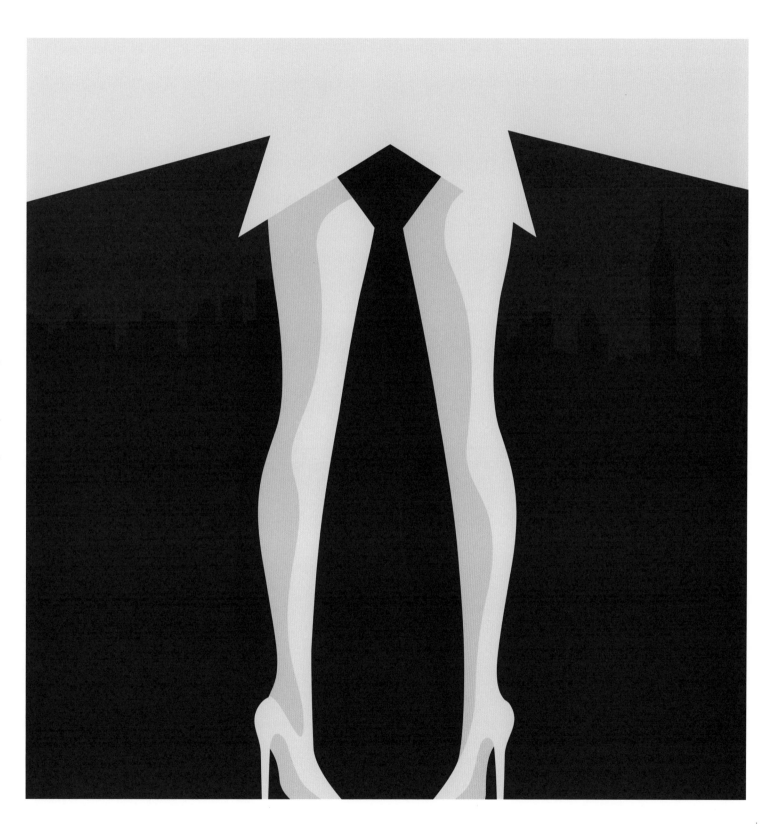

Mad Men, for Empire Review, 2015

In 2013 Transport for London (TfL) commissioned Noma and nine other UK-based designers and studios to produce limited-edition ticket wallets to mark the London Design Festival and the 150th birthday of the London Underground. Noma created a design with a narrative that celebrated the network's forgotten areas, encouraging travellers to look at the iconic logo in a different way and discover a new story within it.

This page and opposite: *Underneath the Underground*, ticket wallet and screenprint, 2013

Celebrate WA is a not-for-profit organization that promotes and runs the annual WA (Western Australia) Day celebrations. In 2015 Noma designed the promotional artwork for the popular State of the Art Festival at the Perth Cultural Centre, which forms part of the WA Day celebrations, and also led an interactive art experience on the day. A brief about relaxation and summer fun naturally led to an illustration of flip-flops or 'thongs'.

Posters for State of the Art Festival. Western Australia, 2015

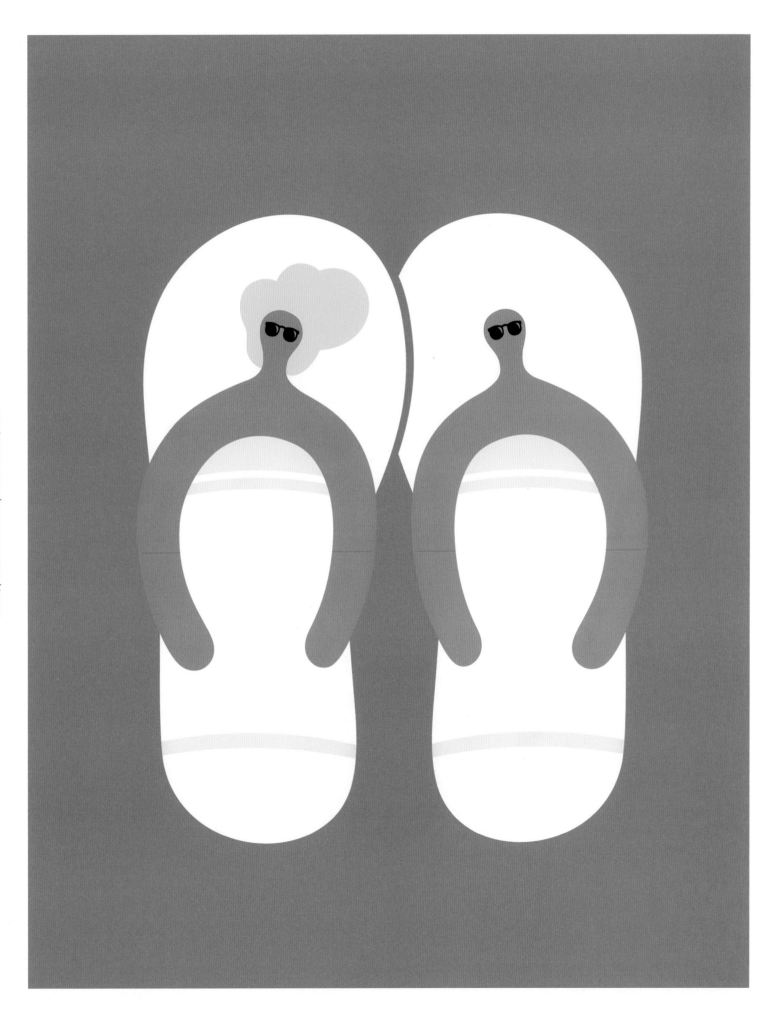

Relax, poster for WA Day celebrations, 2015

Over three years Noma made many images for the Victoria and Albert Museum, and for its education department, inspired by its staggering and wide-ranging collections. They were used to advertise the museum's diverse range of events, lectures and courses, and featured on posters and postcards. Noma's appealing images of animals rather than people sidestep all questions of gender and race, and were chosen by *Creative Review* to appear in its annual round-up of design work in 2010.

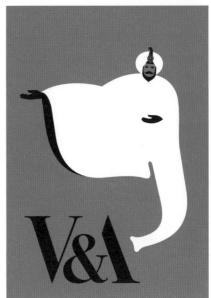

This page and opposite: Posters for the Victoria and Albert Museum, London, 2009–11

66 I combined Japan-inspired visual cues – the hairstyle, the distinctive beard, the colour red – to make this label for Kirin. It's an unusual pleasure to be given such a plain label, and in the end the only lettering to appear on it was the name of the beer itself. **99**

The brief for this design, which was launched at Tokyo Design Week, was 'afternoon beer'. The drink was a sophisticated summer edition blond beer, to be sold in a special box with another 'artist's bottle' and a booklet.

Swing the Mood, special-edition label for Kirin summer beer, 2015

Happy Birthday Playmobil, cover for *De Volkskrant*, Netherlands, 1 December 2012

Amsterdam Design Week, cover for *De Volkskrant*, Netherlands, 19 October 2013

66 I love Dutch art and design, and I get incredible exposure on the covers of the country's main newspapers (*Vrij Nederland* and *De Volkskrant*). Just as the *New York Times* and *The Guardian* do, they fully understand the power of 'less', and appreciate the scale and boldness of my art. Dutch designers are masters of grids and understand their importance – the time I spent studying magazine design really brought this home to me – so for me it is a dream come true to work with a Dutch magazine. **99**

The tulip, which has become a symbol of the Netherlands, forms part of this stylized cover for the Dutch newspaper *De Volkskrant*. It marked a special edition for Amsterdam Design Week, featuring covers by seven different artists.

《

De Volkskrant asked various artists and photographers to contribute to a special issue celebrating the German toymaker Playmobil's fortieth anniversary. Noma's image references the distinctive zigzag hairstyle of the plastic figures and the affection in which the brand is held worldwide, and won the SPD (Society of Publication Designers) award for the best cover design in 2013.

Poster for Opel's 'Umparken im Kopf' (U-Turn in your Head) campaign, 2014

The brief for the illustration below was the idea that beauty is in the eye of the beholder. In the article itself, on our lifelong obsession with beauty, the writer Will Self suggested that the only cure was love. As he put it, love restricts our field of vision 'until, instead of gazing on a vast field of daffodils, we are content, for hour upon hour, to contemplate a single flower'.

《

This cross-media campaign was aimed at debunking all kinds of prejudice and popular misapprehensions about the car brand Opel in Germany. The one shown here was: 'For 100 years, it was thought that spinach was high in iron: until someone measured again.' The campaign was particularly effective because it was at first anonymous, so that Germans were left scratching their heads until the brand's identity was finally revealed. It won a Red Dot award in 2015.

The Art of Wearing a Hat, for GQ France, May 2010

Out in the Cold, for GQ France, September 2011

63

In 2012 Noma moved into three dimensions to make these room sets for *Wallpaper**. To illustrate eight special covers for the magazine's 'Global Design' issue, he was commissioned to create 'rooms' in a studio, featuring products from each chosen territory. Chairs by Jean Nouvel become eyes on the French cover; an ink box by Babaghuri becomes the lips for Japan; and the Norwegian designer Andreas Engesvik's candleholder perfects the smile of the Scandinavian polar bear. The covers were so popular that they were subsequently turned into limited-edition prints and posters.

Spain, cover for Wallpaper, 2012

Scandinavia cover for Wallpaper* 2012

Japan, cover for Wallpaper*, 2012

USA, cover for *Wallpaper**, 2012

69

Bear Hugs, screenprint, 2011

Evolutionary Thought II, screenprint, 2013

Noma created about forty images for the American website iShares, which offers advice for investors. The illustration below was commissioned for an article on looking for suitable investments. Meanwhile, the gossiping friends opposite appeared with an article on the reality of friendship, in which the writer pointed out that many of us don't know our friends as well as we think. 'Perhaps a true friend is someone who doesn't ask many awkward questions,' he concluded. The image has become a popular screenprint in its own right.

Look Again, for iShares, Italy, 2015

Tea for Two, for *The Guardian*, 5 December 2009

This page and opposite: Illustrations for Oliver Burkeman, 'This Column Will Change your Life,' *The Guardian*, 2009–11

There was an unwritten agreement behind these weekly illustrations, that each should be a portrait reflecting a mood, story or thought. This provided some of Noma's most useful training in portraiture, as he depicted his friends or people he saw near his home in north London.

In 2009 Avery, a family dog, strayed and was taken to a shelter. Her owners didn't have the cash to get her out, so an employee promised to put a 'hold for owner' tag on her. Somehow, she was put down. The owners sued for 'sentimental or intrinsic' damages because Avery had little market value but was irreplaceable. The case was dismissed: the court ruled that no one in Texas can recover 'emotion-based' damages.

«

In the battle for public funding, 'the arts sector will lose out unless it can tell a richer story about the benefits it brings,' John Knell explained in the article that accompanied the image opposite. 'Art is not just there for itself. It helps us to re-imagine the good life in the good society.'

The Case of the Priceless Puppy, for Reader's Digest, USA, March 2015

The tongue-in-cheek illustration below, for *GQ France*, poked fun at the art world by implying that not all works are as important as critics might suggest.

Modern Art Critic for GQ France, August 2012

»

A humourless-looking chap in a top hat introduces this French book of British humour, but perhaps he is just disgruntled because a pigeon has misbehaved on his umbrella. The book featured a selection of anecdotes, quotations, riddles and humorous verse from British comedians, intentional and unintentional, all presented with a translation and cultural commentary.

Cover for *Le Grand Livre de l'Humour British* (The Big Book of British Humour), Assimil, 2013

Problem Solved I for Dragon Rouge, Business Is Beautiful 2012

82 Craft for Dragon Rouge Business Is Beautiful 2009

Cover for Dragon Rouge, *Business is Beautiful*, 2012

The American company Lyft commissioned Noma to produce these images for large murals, animations, outdoor advertising and print ads in an attempt to raise awareness of the idea of car-sharing. The illustrations focused on the playful side of transport and the freedom of car-sharing, which has environmental as well as financial benefits. Below, clockwise from top left, are *Nice Approach*, *Do the Ride Thing*, *Hop to It*, *Roll Out*, *Wheel and Deal* and *Rides on Tap*.

This page and opposite: Illustrations for Lyft advertising campaign, 2016

These designs for English courses aimed at French speakers incorporated a speech bubble into objects that are traditionally associated with England, such as the bowler hat and the black cab. For the illustration opposite, Noma played with the most widely recognized symbols of London, integrating them with the idea of speech and communication.

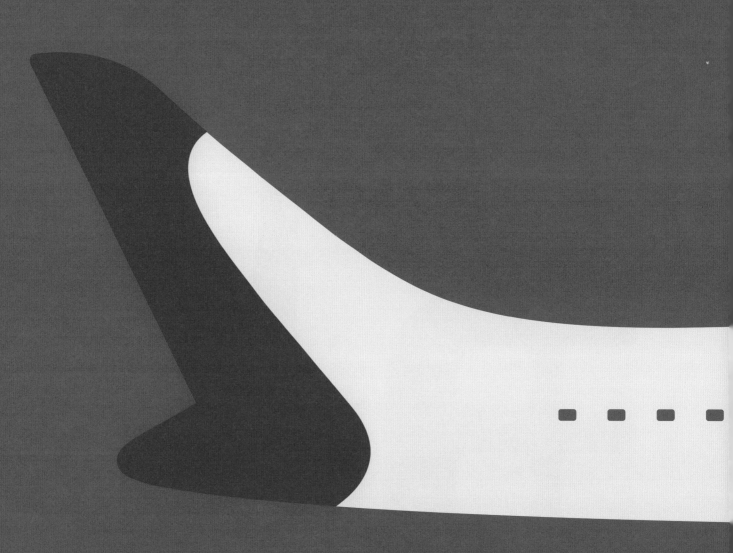

'The Smart Alternative' campaign, extra legroom for business-class travellers, Air Berlin, March 2016

Surrealism | poster for Garage Museum of Contemporary Art Moscow 2010

Surrealism II, poster for Garage Museum of Contemporary Art, Moscow, 2011

I love urban walks, and I'm always happy to get lost in big cities. On a walk in Seville, I found a dusty black metal cycling sign on the ground (below). All his friends were set firmly in the pavement, but he was just lying there. I cleaned off the black dust and discovered a beautiful 'baby John Lennon' that looked at me and asked in Spanish if I would take him to my studio and put him on my shelf. I couldn't refuse. "

Noma's found cycling sign was soon able to provide the inspiration for an illustration commissioned by the British magazine *Cycling Plus*. The article, on safety, examined the difficulties faced by local authorities and road planners in terms of how to protect cyclists from drivers.

Be Safe Out There, for Cycling Plus, September 2013

The German edition of *Wired* magazine gave Noma an open brief on the subject of creativity and finding ideas. The resulting image compares the process of finding that winning idea to a mouse sniffing out a piece of cheese – it may be hard to find, but each new discovery is a reward.

»

Africa, although rich in resources, has issues with power. This article examined the pros and cons of the various solutions. The many ideas for sustainable power generation are shown by the light bulb, but the giraffe reminds us of Africa's natural riches and inhabitants, and the care that must be taken to protect them.

Men's Fitness asked Noma to create a monthly illustration for its business section. The image below, on the left, was made for an article on wisdom in investing, through the story of a Wall Street investor/philosopher who believes conventional attitudes to investing are wrong. The image on the right expresses a much more conventional view of the stock market; a bull market is traditionally one that is strong and rising, while a bear market is the opposite.

Illustrations for Men's Fitness 2014 and 2016

> **❝** I met the American graphic designer Lance Wyman recently. I love his pictograms for the 1968 Olympic Games in Mexico City, so I decided to create my own Paralympic version. **❞**

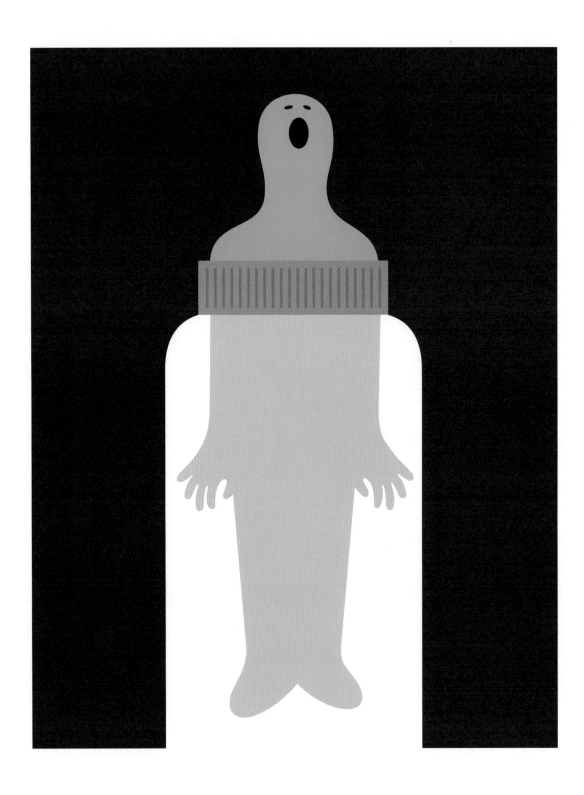

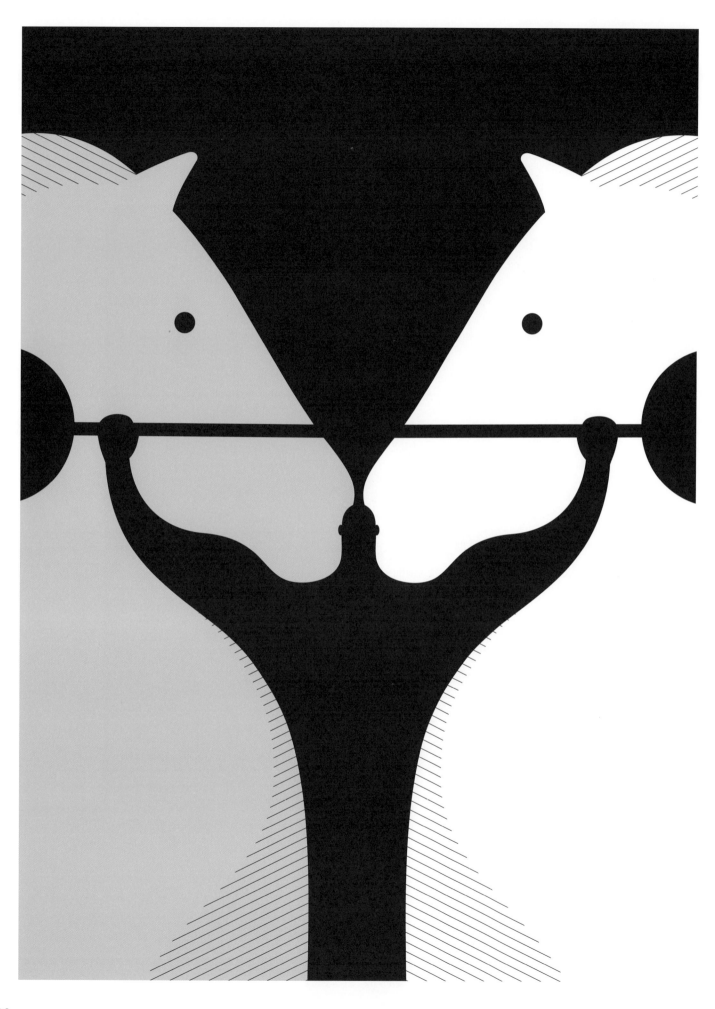

Horse Power, screenprint, 2013

The *New York Times* ran an article about a study that suggested Tetris might help the victims of traumatic events, who are prone to flashbacks. This intensely visual game occupies the brain to such an extent that it has no spare capacity to record or replay recent traumatic events or images, resulting in a much lower rate of PTSD-related symptoms.

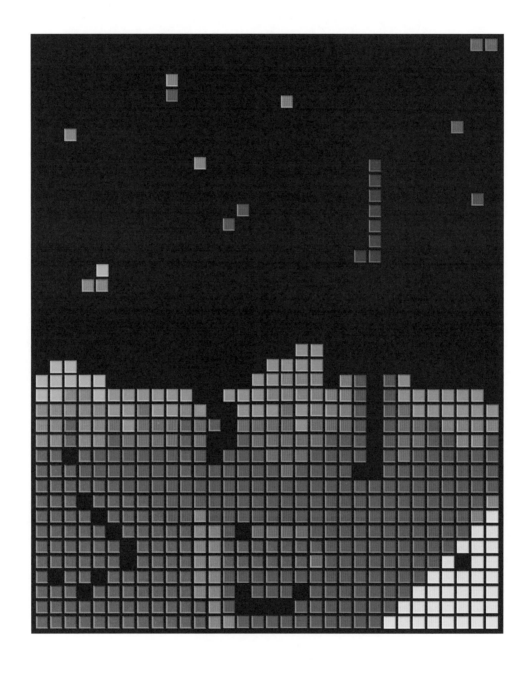

Treating PTSD for the New York Times 13 December 2009

This image was for a story about nutrition, comparing cultivated fruit and vegetables and their wild equivalents. Our love of sweet tastes has meant that crops have become much less nutritionally valuable.

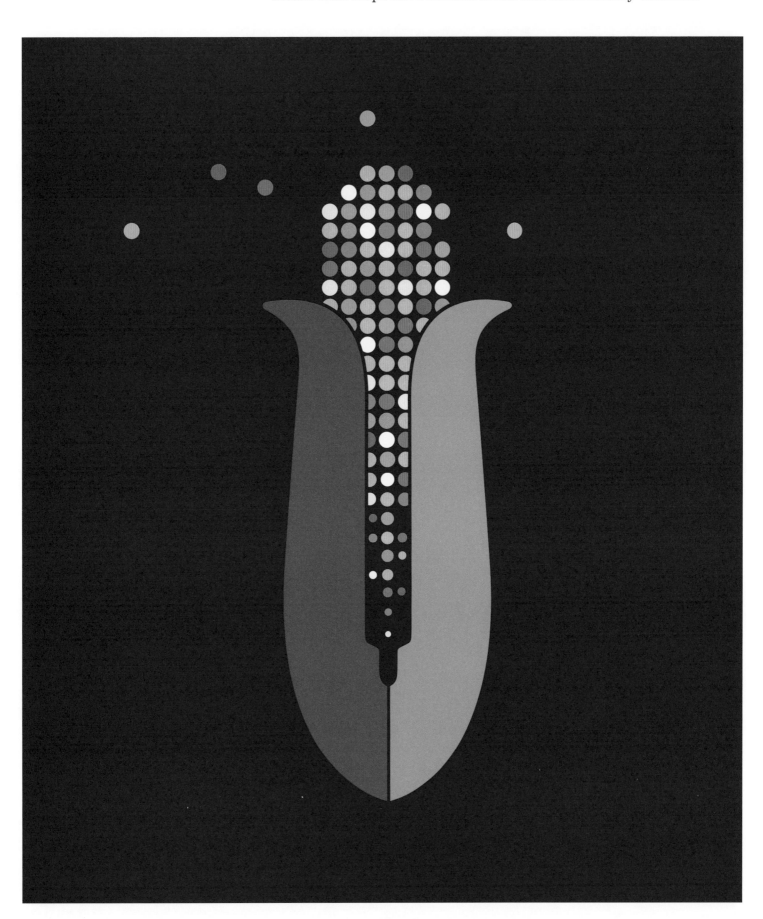

Breeding out the Goodness, for the New York Times Sunday Review, 26 May 2013

“ One rainy day in Old Street, London,
I saw an abandoned, beaten umbrella on
the pavement. It looked like Concorde and
made me feel like escaping the weather.
I sketched it in the rain, and a few months
later I had made it into a screenprint and
exhibited it in my solo show, 'Bitter Sweet',
at KK Outlet, London (2010). ”

Escape the Weather, screenprint, 2010

Dialogue, cover for *Werte-Index*, 2014

This page and opposite: *Bird's-Eye View*, for Momotuku Ando cultural foundation, Japan, 2015

66 Something seen in a strange way started me off on this project, and the bird-like folded leaves that had caught my interest became a bird-shaped tree house in shades of green. I called it *Bird's-Eye View*. It's wonderful to be able to extend my visual storytelling to a larger scale, to move from illustration into architecture. 99

This bird-shaped wooden pavilion set among trees was commissioned by the Momofuku Ando cultural foundation to form a lookout at the highest point of a wood in Nagano Prefecture, central Japan. Through the foundation's Tree House project many such structures have been commissioned and built, but Noma is so far the only non-Japanese artist to have participated. The shape and colour of the 9-metre-high (30-ft) structure are inspired by folded leaves, but its silhouette is that of a bird. The experience of discovery as the viewer approaches – is it a large leaf, or is it about to take flight like a bird? – continues on the small, sheltered platform, from which views extend over the trees towards the active volcano Mount Asama. It was built by a team of twenty Japanese carpenters, and is anchored to the ground by a cherry-tree stump at one end and a column at the foot of the stairs.

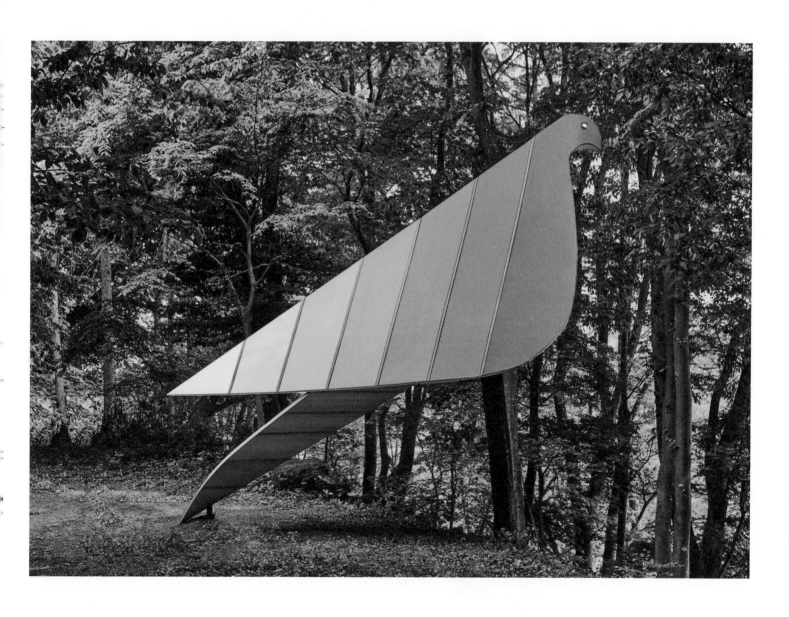

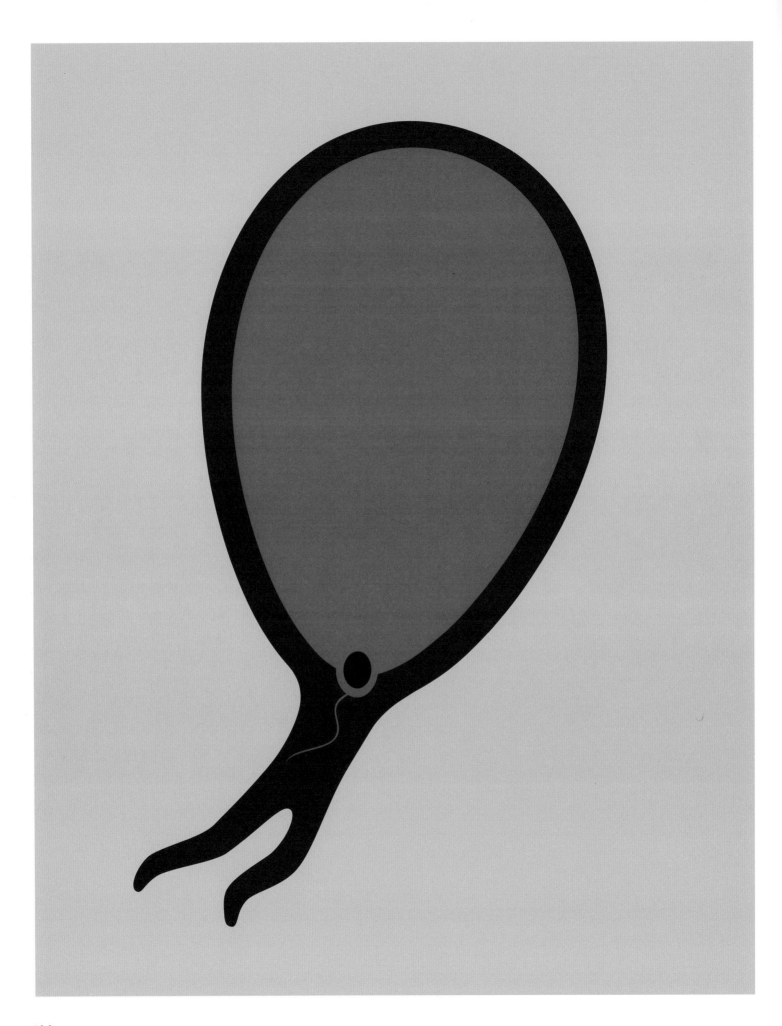

Mouse vs. Pencil, poster for MU&ST Festival, Italy, 2013

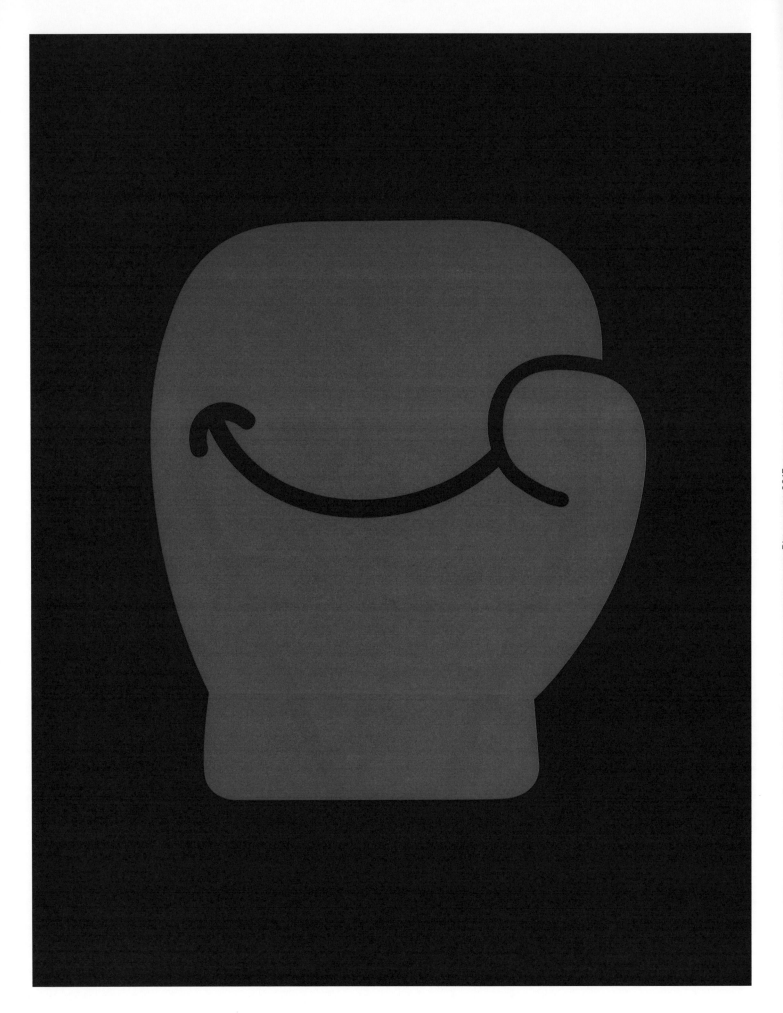

The publication of *The Story of Emoji* by Gavin Lucas coincided with an exhibition of the same name at the KK Outlet gallery in London in 2016. As part of the project, various contemporary designers were asked to produce original emojis that they wished existed. The one below by Noma symbolizes a hangover.

The illustration opposite was made for an adult story based on the tale of Little Red Riding Hood for *GQ* magazine in 2008. In the end the editor chose another of Noma's submissions, but this image has since become iconic, and is used by design universities around the world as a teaching aid. Later it appeared on the cover of *Piauí* and was released as a limited-edition screenprint.

The magazine *Wallpaper** brought out a discovery-themed supplement celebrating everything the Netherlands has to offer. Noma's mirror-image cover (below) features many of the country's most distinctive buildings, including the spectacular NEMO Science Museum in Amsterdam. The image was subsequently picked up by the Dutch tourist board.

Cover for Wallpaper* 'Dutch Discovery' supplement, January 2006

»

In 2009 the Royal Academy held an exhibition called 'Paper City: Urban Utopias', displaying the various contributions to *Blueprint*'s regular back-page feature 'Paper City'. Noma's illustration celebrated the street sign as a vital part of the cityscape and the effective use of urban space.

Collaboration poster for Sales, 1 2006

116

Fatal Attraction, screenprint, 2009

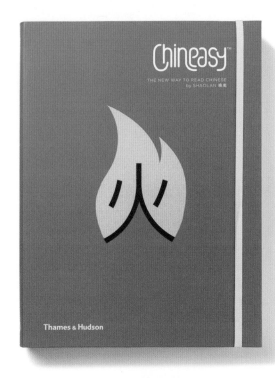

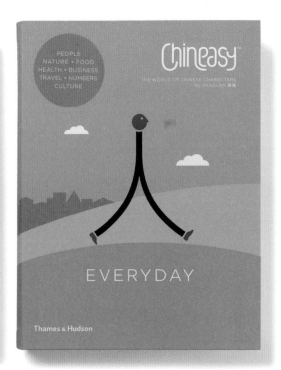

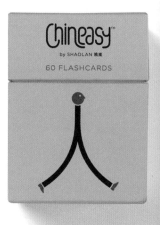

Chineasy

Having studied Hebrew type design at college, Noma had a keen interest in typography, but when he moved to London he felt 'lost in translation'. Unable to express himself with the ease or creativity of his native language, he started drawing facial expressions instead. His language became visual and featured no type at all.

Chineasy brought Noma back to type. Developed by the tech entrepreneur ShaoLan Hsueh, who could not find a good way of teaching her children Chinese, it is a groundbreaking visual approach to teaching basic building blocks to give a rapid understanding of the language. The illustration process involved Skype chats in which ShaoLan would tell old stories about the connotations of each character. Noma then went to the woods as usual to sketch, offering ideas from a Western point of view. ShaoLan chose those that best represented each character, after which Noma would redraw them, checking the angles and colours. Each effortless-looking character was in fact drawn many times.

The two *Chineasy* books were published in 2014 and 2016; they have been translated into numerous languages and are used by many schools. In 2014 *Chineasy* was nominated for design of the year by the Design Museum in London, and won *Wallpaper** magazine's Lifechanger award. In 2015 it won two D&AD wooden pencils, and the illustrations were honoured with a YCN (You Can Now) Gold Bar.

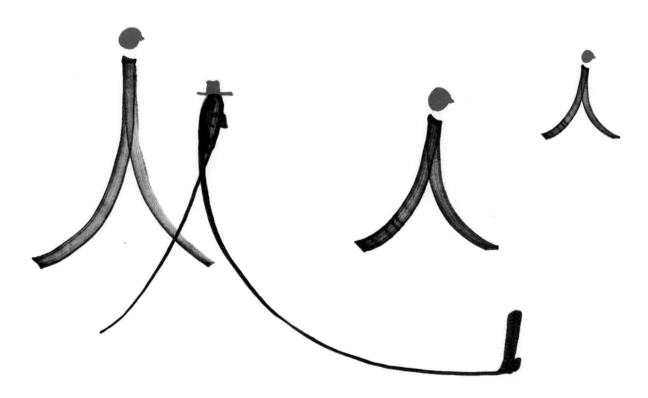

66 *Chineasy* took me back to type again, not as a type designer, but more as an explorer and inventor. From the start, when ShaoLan sent me the very first characters, I knew the type would be in the centre and that my illustration would dance around it. The Chinese character is nearly always black, and my drawing – whether behind it, around it or inside it – whispers or shouts its meaning. The Homer Simpson character below wasn't used in the end, but these two illustrations show just how flexible the *Chineasy* system is. I liked the idea of using Homer because he is also an anti-dad, but in the end we chose the more competent-looking man opposite. **99**

66 In the *Chineasy* method, simple building blocks such as those shown here are used in various combinations to provide the foundation for words, phrases and even complete stories. 99

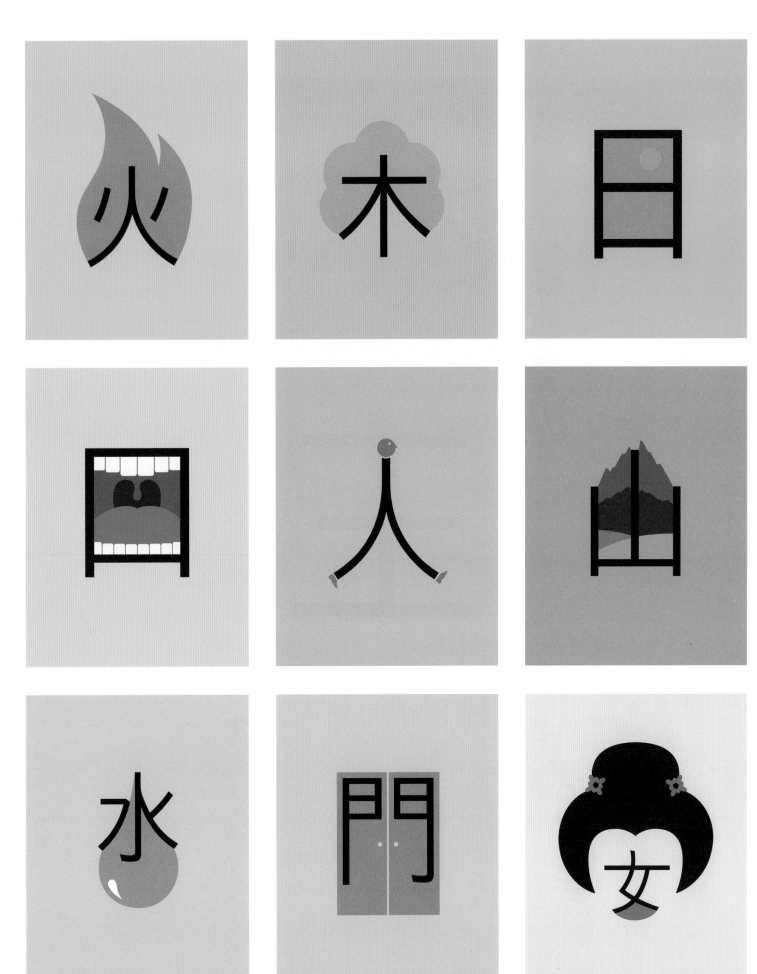

Left to right, from top: 'Fire', 'Tree', 'Sun', 'Mouth', 'Person', 'Mountain', 'Water', 'Door' and 'woman', Chineasy, 2014

'King' (this page) and 'Master' (opposite) characters, *Chineasy*, 2016

The children's piece *Peter and the Wolf*, for orchestra and narrator, was written by the Russian composer Sergei Prokofiev in 1936. Noma created smooth, curved landscapes that would support the Chinese characters to tell the story. This storytelling experience appears in the final pages of the first *Chineasy* book, and it also influenced the spread approach in the second book. So far, it is the only time a *Chineasy* character has appeared in any colour other than black.

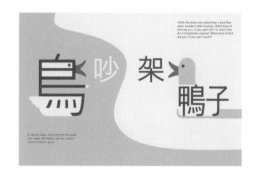
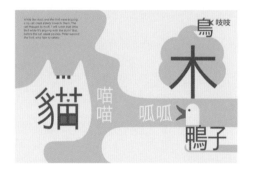
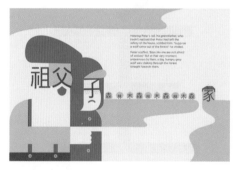

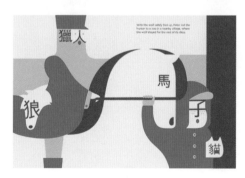

彼得與狼
The Story of Peter and the Wolf

IN

OUT

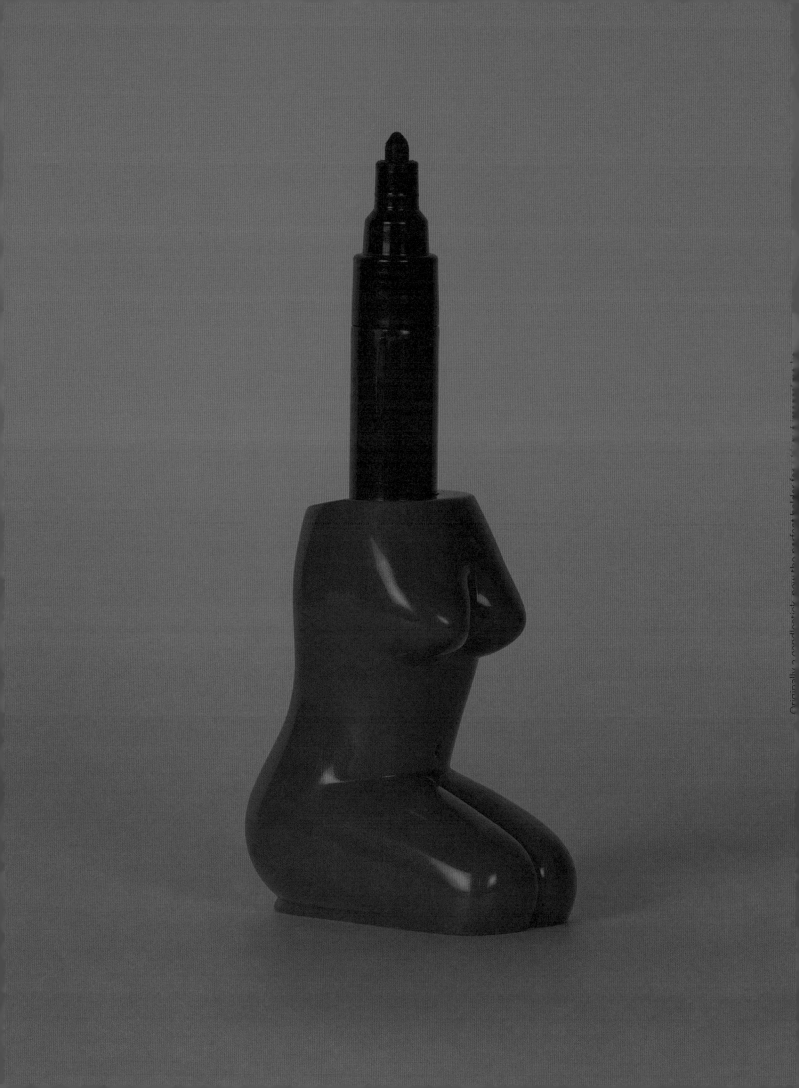

Originally a candlestick, now the perfect holder for ...

In common with many kids of the 1970s, I made my first sexual discovery through the pages of magazines. My schoolmate Iris once took some of us into her parents' bedroom, where she showed us her father's treasure: a large collection of *Bul* magazines hidden in his cabinet. I still remember the logo, an arrow hitting a target in the centre (*bul* means 'accurate' in Hebrew). It was the first Hebrew erotic publication, dating from the 1960s, naive and beautiful, full of black-and-white images of minimally clothed Swedish and German women in exciting positions that we had never even thought of before. We decided to share our knowledge with our friends, so we took the pile of magazines away with us. Unfortunately the enthusiasm of our classmates was such that all the magazines were snapped up and, to Iris's horror, we lost control of who had what. . .

Some twenty-five years later I'm working in print and online, to briefs from *The Guardian*, *GQ*, *Esquire*, *The Times*, Channel 4 and other international media. The naive sharing of magazines among my school friends has transformed into digital sharing, and explicit information and images are accessible to everyone. They're super-realistic and extreme, and I can't ignore them, but only offer my own point of view. Sex is a sensitive subject, and it seems to me that illustration is a great way to deal with that sensitivity. A lot of my illustrations give the impression of personifying body parts, which I think brings the viewer closer to the subject matter. Modern discussions about sex – not to mention the pornographic images and videos that are so easily available online – have become competitive, idealized and depersonalized, and it's my aim to increase sympathy and identification with these sometimes tricky topics. I'm trying to inject the playfulness and imagination that I feel we have lost in our hyper-digital life, and if I can prompt a chuckle as someone reads an article about an embarrassing problem, so much the better.

I don't choose the subjects I work on for magazines and newspapers; they come to me. I think perhaps the editors choose me for these topics because as well as being quite sensitive, my work is fairly abstract. It's a way of getting at a subject like sex without being too literal. For example, I think my illustration for the article on penis size (page 194) represents a real change in editorial illustration. Many editors might have chosen a coy photograph of a depressed-looking man with his head in his hands, but *The Guardian* went for my image despite being a mainstream publication. They would never have run a photograph of a penis – undersized or otherwise – but my illustration tells the story in a different way, with positivity and a softer touch. It makes me smile every time I see it.

Having a small penis may be a matter of concern to the man in question, but there are many sexual topics that are very serious in a more far-reaching way, from suspected paedophilia and rape during war to infertility and homophobia. Again, I find that a light – though never belittling – approach strikes a chord with editors and readers, since it is difficult for all of us, me included, to contemplate these things.

I was lucky enough to work for a few years with Maïa Mazaurette on her sex column for *GQ France*, and many of those artworks are illustrated in this book. Her writing is direct and realistic, and everything comes from her own experience. She shared her expertise and tips candidly with the readers of *GQ*, and my illustrations supported her stories. Mazaurette's is an attitude that I think can really help discussions of sex in the modern world: no-nonsense, down-to-earth and uncompromising, yet with an open mind and free of judgment.

Some of my images are explicit, but others have to be a little more oblique, such as the screenprints for the Lutyens restaurant in London (see pages 140–41). Mine was the second set of artworks to be commissioned specially for this new establishment, and they were to hang in the public space. I played with the idea of 'full-bodied' in its wine-related meaning and also in terms of the female form, but it's only on closer examination that you might see anything to do with sex at all.

Many illustrations become stronger in partnership with an article or interview, but I'm particularly fond of those that need no explanation at all, not even a title. These are the ones I choose most often for gallery shows, since they are effective out of their original editorial context. I think of it as 'silent storytelling'.

In Out is a journey over the human body and human relationships, exploring our own personal negative spaces and rebutting negative attitudes to what should be positive experiences. Women have nine body openings, men eight, and we grow in our mother's biggest negative space, the womb, as a result of penetration. When I make my illustrations, I go inside negative spaces and reinvent them, and we too are created by ins and outs. That is surely the most positive experience of all.

By the way, Iris needn't have worried: her father never said a word. The next day after dinner, he was stroking the family's poodle, cheekily accusing it of chewing his slippers and opening his cabinet.

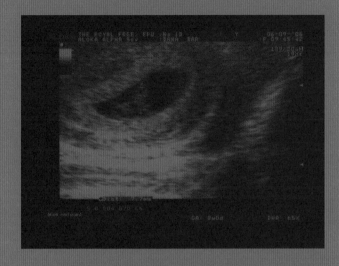
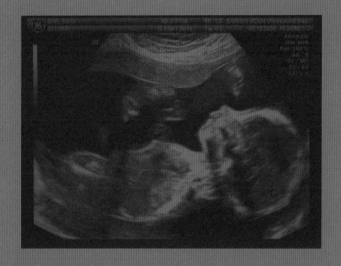
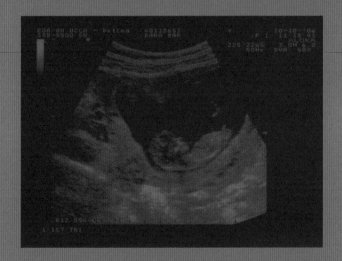
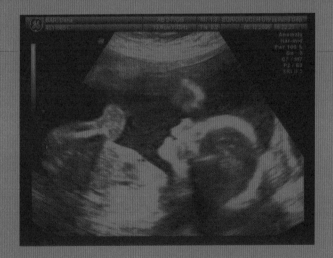

With or Without You, wood and metal sculpture, 2010

Talking about Sex, for GQ France, June 2010

> 66 When I started to sketch I realized that a classic zip can form the shape and contour of female legs, and that the negative space at the top of the zip can suggest the vagina. When the zip is open the legs are open, and we then make that discovery. I like this duality, the movement and the chain reaction caused by the actions. 99

Penguin commissioned Noma to produce a cover for the fortieth-anniversary reissue of the cult 1970s novel *Fear of Flying* by Erica Jong. This powerful yet slightly naive image evoked the sexually liberated female mind, with the symbolic use of the zip and female form creating a narrative. It was selected by the *New York Times* as one of the best covers of 2013, and was also celebrated in Paul Buckley's book *Classic Penguin: Cover to Cover* (2016), in which Jong herself wrote that she was 'delighted' with Noma's illustration: '[It] suggests an exuberant and sexual woman. Behind that exuberance is a full mind and imaginative talents that need to be expressed . . . The most important thing about my heroines . . . is that they are full human beings.'

Scientists at the University of Oxford published a paper suggesting that, at some point fairly soon, a new breed of 'love drug' might become available – a medication that could heal wounded relationships. Noma created this illustration for an article by Will Storr that reported on their findings.

Full-Bodied I, for Prescott & Conran's Conran's Lustrware, Ltd., Lyon, screenprint, 2016

Full-Bodied II, for Prescott & Conran's Lutyens restaurant, screenprint, 2014

In 2009 the new owner of the *Erotic Review* claimed that women are not capable of writing effective, sexually explicit full-frontal erotica. The writer Kathy Lette responded in passionate repudiation of such an idea on the front page of the *Times Saturday Review*.

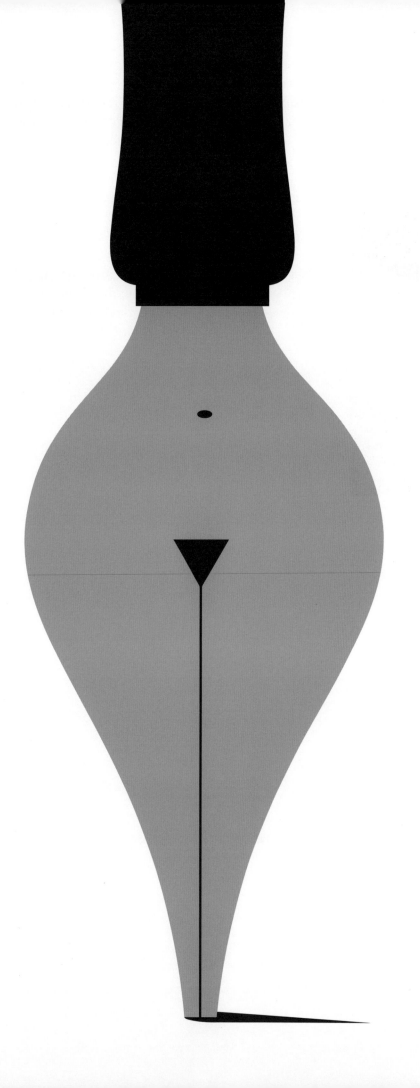

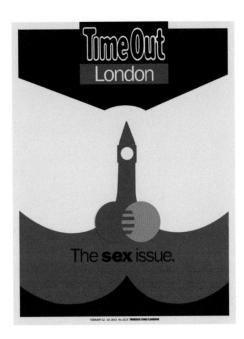

Time Out London commissioned Noma to create a graphic image to adorn the cover of its special sex-themed issue. He came up with this composition featuring one of London's most famous landmarks, the clock tower of the Houses of Parliament, known as Big Ben. However, an advertiser bought the cover position at the very last minute and did not want to be associated with sexual imagery. Noma designed a version that incorporated the sponsor's logo (left), but in the end the image was pulled from the printed edition. Instead, the magazine ran a blank cover to launch a competition that encouraged readers to create and tweet their own 'sexy' covers. As *Creative Review* put it in an article on the surprise cover, 'perhaps Bar's image was just too much for the travelling public?' The issue came out just a few months before *Time Out* became a free magazine, and fuelled the debate over whether the increased reliance on advertisers would give them extra creative clout.

These illustrations accompanied articles on women's use of the internet to administer their love lives, whether for online flirting (below) or in the form of sex hook-up sites (opposite). In an age of instant gratification, many women are looking not for Mr Right but for Mr Right Now.

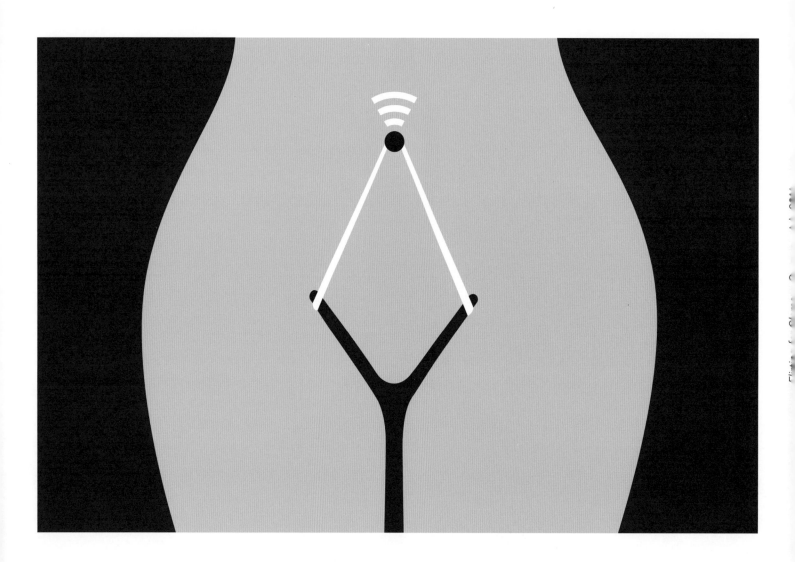

The penis can be compared with a well-trained dog, according to Mels van Driel, senior urologist at the Groningen University Medical Centre and author of the amusingly titled *Manhood: The Rise and Fall of the Penis* (2009). For *Esquire* magazine, Van Driel compiled a list of thirteen facts about 'man's real best friend', including several things no one in their right mind would want to know, such as frightening information about penis fractures, medieval penis curses and hypospadias, a penile abnormality that affects one in 200 men.

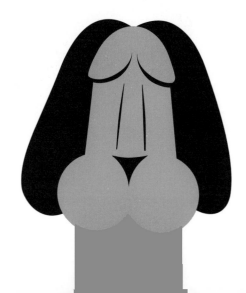

Noma produced this illustration for an article that examined women's habits when it comes to talking about sex: whether they find it easy, who they do it with and how much detail they go into.

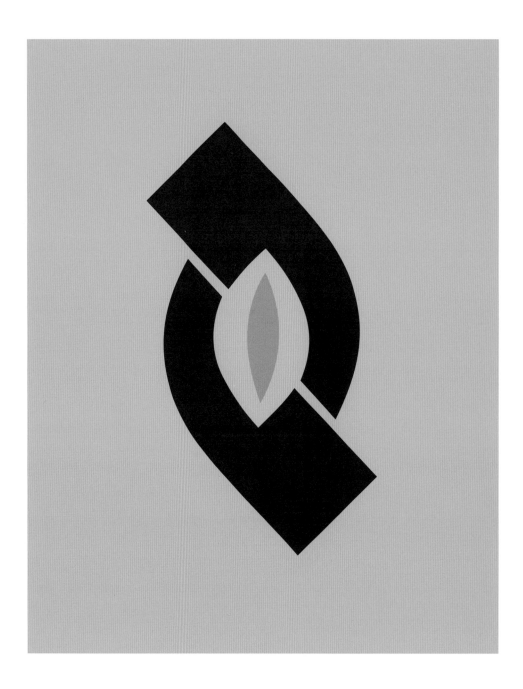

This image accompanied a men's guide to sexting, which described the mobile phone as a new erogenous zone. The writer listed various dos (be patient when waiting for a reply, consider your timing, and so on) and such enlightening don'ts as 'don't send a photo of your penis. EVER': quite apart from being used against you during the relationship and by the bad-taste police, it may end up being seen by your employer or the divorce court.

These images illustrated a piece by the sex columnist Maïa Mazaurette about learning how to enjoy being pinned down in conversation by beautiful women who have no interest in you beyond flirting and teasing.

This page and opposite: *Pin Me Down*, for GQ France, June 2014

This naughty 'P' accompanied a magazine feature that explored how the actress Pamela Anderson balanced her sexy image with a canny business acumen.

GQ France commissioned this image for a piece on the complex psychological factors that govern our attraction to wealthy partners. The writer brought in the subject of Social Darwinism to suggest that those who are perceived as strong and successful will always be sought after as partners.

This article made clear the sad truth that, in terms of sex and desire, being a nice guy is useless. Men must be aggressive, ruthless, almost rude – proper 'bad boys' – if they want to get laid, according to the female writer.

Rise of the Bad Boy, for GQ France, March 2011

These illustrations were commissioned for an article about the internationally recognized Thai surgeon Dr Preecha, who is known as the 'vagina king' and the 'godfather' of transgender surgery.

This page and opposite: The Vagina King for De Volkskrant, Netherlands, 2015

Noma produced this illustration for an article on S&M, which warned men that although many women are in favour of it, it is important to find out for definite before trying anything tough. Particularly crucial is the ability to tell the difference between simulated rejection, which is part of the act, and true rejection and fear.

To accompany a piece by John von Sothen about modern attitudes to cheating, Noma combined the Playboy bunny with a pair of blood-stained scissors, bringing to mind the notorious case of Lorena Bobbitt, who famously chopped off her unfaithful and allegedly abusive husband's penis in 1993.

These two images were commissioned for a feature in which the journalist Rachel Aviv asked if it is right to imprison people for heinous crimes they have not yet committed. It looked at the case of a former US soldier who was imprisoned for years for storing child pornography on his computer, even though he had never been found to commit a sexual offence with a youngster.

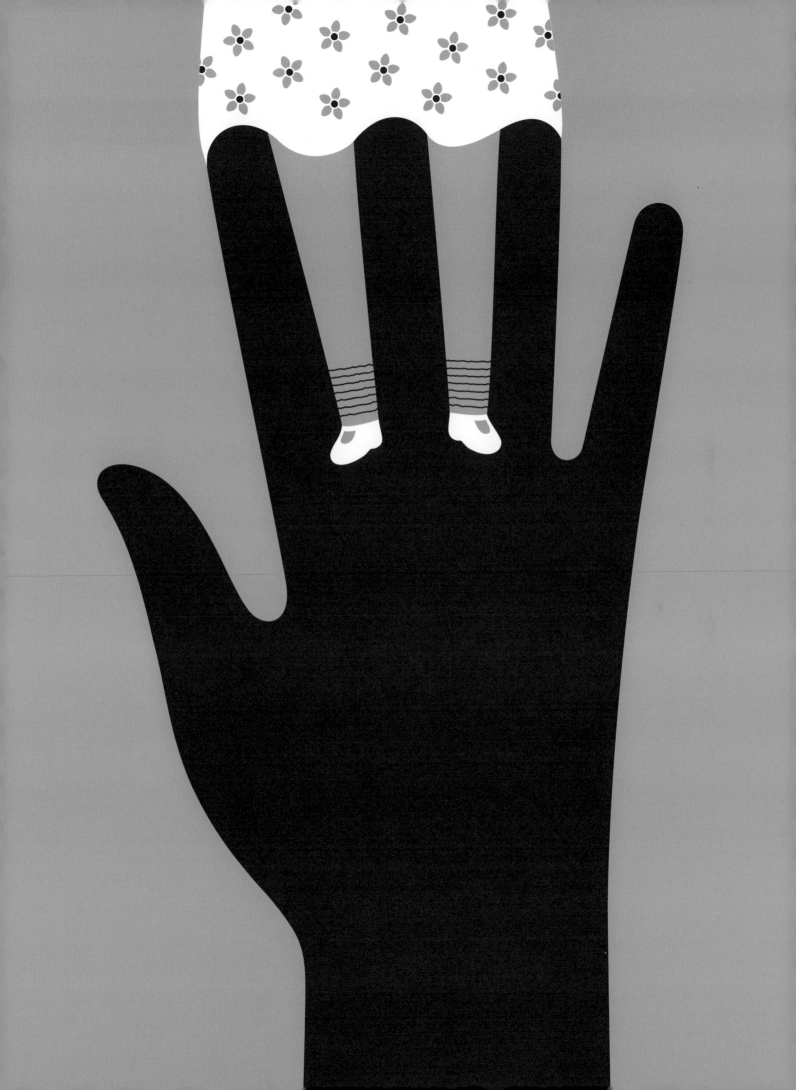

This image was created for a book about stalking, 'when the refusal to be refused leads to violence'. The authors examined what causes such behaviour and explained how we can best protect ourselves from it. As an image, it is one of Noma's simplest, but the graphic representation of a stranger looking over one's shoulder is quietly chilling.

Taking threesomes as her subject, the sexpert Maïa Mazaurette explained that this common male fantasy is pretty difficult to organize in real life. She suggested that the man allow the women to take the initiative, and that he please both of them equally. But ultimately, she said, if you don't feel up to the task, forget about it.

The radio programme *Sugar Daddy, Sugar Baby* on BBC Radio 4 met the young women who are funding their university courses and covering their living costs by making 'arrangements' with wealthy older men. Such arrangements often – but not always – involve a physical relationship. It seems the idea of the 'sugar daddy' has been updated, however, as the women interviewed clearly felt very strongly in control, and many felt the 'relationship' was conducted entirely on their own terms.

Pillow Talk, 2010

Channel 4's 'Mating Season' was a series of programmes about twenty-first-century dating. To promote the shows, Noma was asked to create a number of icons for a glossary that highlighted the complications of modern dating. The symbols refer to a host of relationship types and sexual preferences, including Textual Relationships, Cuddling (cuddle parties are, apparently, a real thing, where guests snuggle their way to meeting new people), Bisexuality, Long Distance, Furring (the wearing of animal costumes to have sex; see opposite) and Threesomes.

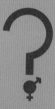

Noma produced this illustration for an article about foreplay. As well as reminding men that foreplay isn't just a prelude to 'real sex', it offered some suggestions for how to do it properly, from a woman's point of view.

These illustrations accompanied an article in which writers and personalities, from the late A.A. Gill to India Knight and Emma Watson, offered advice and opinion on the trials of Valentine's Day, and recalled some of their favourite (or not) celebrations.

Fun and laughter seem to be on the decline in our sexual relationships and encounters, and 'weird' sex acts and practices are being made fun of by people who consider themselves to be 'normal' (or perhaps boring), according to the article for which the illustration below was commissioned. During the 1980s and 1990s, porn actors might well laugh out loud during a scene, something that is unthinkable now. The writer advised us all to be a bit less dramatic and serious during sex.

»

In another column in *GQ France*, men were asked to think more about their own pleasure, rather than focusing on giving orgasms to their female partners. They should explore their own bodies and sensations, and try to be a little more secure about being touched in places other than the obvious.

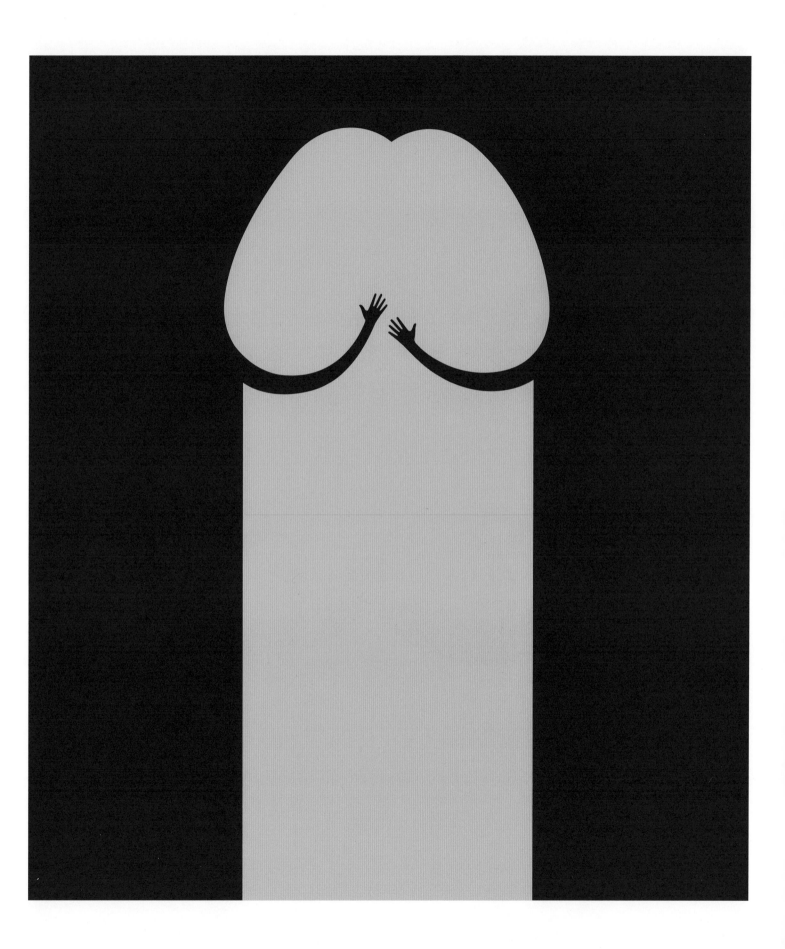

184

In 2009 Iceland introduced fines and jail sentences for anyone caught using prostitutes, and in 2010 it outlawed strip clubs. These two illustrations appeared in a piece in *The Economist* looking at the Icelandic government's attempts to ban violent online pornography, and questioning the country's ability to define, regulate and police such legislation.

These images were produced for *GQ France*'s special supplement '100 Things Men Should Know about Sex'. The crucial advice included what to do straight afterwards (don't ask for feedback, whatever you do); what to think about in order not to come too soon (among the suggestions: Carla Bruni's next album, Fukushima's mutant spiders and the situation in the Middle East); and whether or not to take control.

 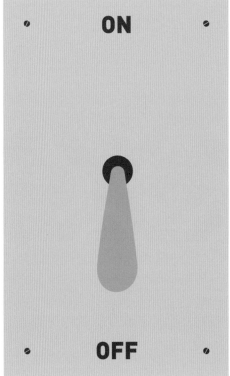 

This page and opposite: 100 Things Men Should Know about Sex, for GQ France, August 2011

What makes a good-looking dick? According to the article for which these illustrations were produced, it's not just about being hard and straight; it also has to look nice when flaccid, and be smooth. Other factors such as cleanliness and hair play a part, but as the article pointed out, beauty means nothing if you don't use it right.

This page and opposite: Good-Looking Dick, for 6a France, 2010

Silicone Valleys for Opella "Apple" vein Knife/Hot-vein-milk-ceramics-art-2014

The illustration below was for an article that asked if 'maintenance sex' exists. Can a man initiate sex if he wants it but his partner doesn't? Is it OK for him not to feel horny when she does? Since sex isn't always intense and multi-orgasmic, the article suggested that readers should enjoy run-of-the-mill sex, low-budget yet pleasant in a B-movie way. But if there's any discrepancy between a man's desire and his partner's, another solution must be found.

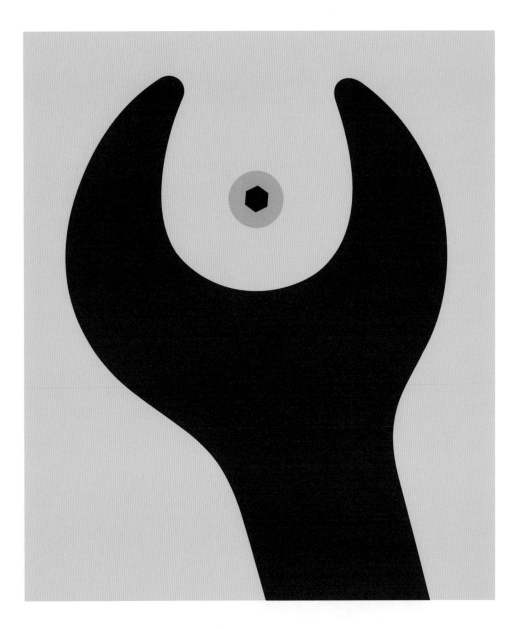

The article for which Noma produced these illustrations centred on the idea that being (and looking) horny can be a good way for a man to turn a woman on. It explored the many ways that a man can show a woman how much he wants her: be verbally explicit, for example, or look at her with your wildest eye and move closer. You shouldn't worry about scaring her off: a direct approach is the perfect way to find out how she feels about it and to work out your next move.

《

Here, the negative space is transformed into a thumb-sized image of a penis, urging a size-anxious man to see himself from a different angle. The image represented a real change for editorial of this kind.

The question of whether or not to kiss and tell is a point of etiquette on which many people stumble, and this article advised the readers of *GQ France* how to respond when quizzed about recent sexual encounters. The consensus was that one should never brag to friends: it's best just to say that it was nice without going into detail.

This image was used alongside a men's guide to the ins and outs of bringing a woman to sexual ecstasy using only the fingers.

Fingering, for GQ France, July 2013

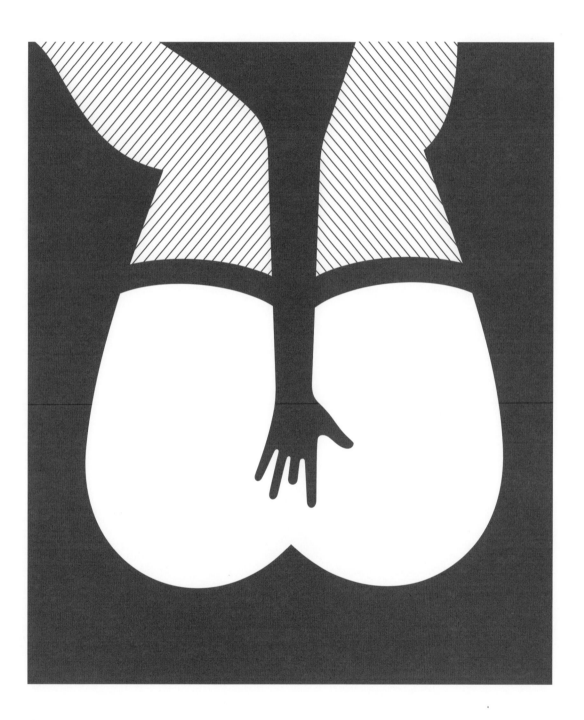

It's fairly obvious which part of the body will give a man most satisfaction, as the writer of this brief explained. Although women don't work in the same way, they know the score, so don't hurry them to touch it. He also counselled against flourishing it suddenly in the manner of a magician pulling a rabbit out of a hat, hence this light-hearted treatment of the subject.

Rabbit in a Hat, unpublished, 2014

PRETTY

UGLY

I have always found human faces attractive and interesting, and enjoyed exploring human expression. I drew my teachers at school; in fact, I used quick horizontal lines so that it would look as though I were writing. That's how I learned to draw and listen at the same time. When I'm chatting, or meeting someone for the first time, I might pull out my sketchbook and draw him or her, or the lady with the dog at the next table or the face hidden in the folds of a coat.

The portrait that really changed things for me came out of a chance encounter with a radioactivity symbol in a bomb shelter during the first Gulf War (see opposite and page 207). That was one of the images I showed people when I moved to London and started to contact magazines and newspapers, looking for work. It's how I got my first commission for *Time Out*, and that was a turning point.

Each portrait presents a new challenge. I always begin with the story of the person, and when I know what I want to say I start to experiment on paper. For editorial portraits, I read the article first to work out the story. I don't trace photos; instead, I look at what motivates the space of the face. I even mimic the expressions in a mirror. I find it astonishing that we all have two eyes, a nose and a mouth and yet no one looks quite like anyone else. The easiest faces are those that are most characterful – such as Quentin Tarantino (page 218), Sylvester Stallone (page 238) and, in a more extreme sense, Stephen Hawking (page 277) – but even the most classically beautiful person in the world has a defining characteristic that, if captured, will make a portrait of them instantly recognizable. Other depictions rely more on props, for example Harry Potter's school tie and famous glasses (pages 246–47) or Indiana Jones's hat (page 222). My portraits are distilled; they are serving a story. Understanding a face is one thing, but getting the story is another.

The portraits I like best are the simplest: my image of Mr Spock (page 225) is one of my favourites, where one little touch tells the whole story. I particularly love floating heads, like those sculpted by the Romanian modernist Constantin Brancusi. For some people, such as Arnold Schwarzenegger (page 265), it is essential to include the neck, but for me the ideal is to show just the head. The shape of the head itself is very important in any portrait I do.

Often I look at faces in an odd way, not just literally (although, with no classical background in portraiture, I do tend to focus on strange things such as the gap between eyes and nose) but also socially. As an incomer in London, I'm not familiar with the local characters and personalities; when I'm talking to someone, I don't know the history or implication of his accent. In my own country it would take me two minutes of conversation to work out everything about a person, but here I am content not to know. I look at everyone in the same way, and being a constant outsider keeps my observation fresh. I like the balance between knowledge and imagination, and the diversity of the city. For me, taking a trip on the Tube is a kaleidoscope of visual excitement: if I get the chance to sit down, there is a constantly changing gallery of six people in the seats opposite. I might concentrate on drawing one, look down to get the shadow of the ear just right, then look up to find that someone else has taken her place, and start drawing his features on the same face.

When it comes to well-known people, it's amazing how the writing affects the finished artwork. I might draw the same person again and again, but the story will change and so the illustration will be different. That has been the case with Saddam Hussein and Harry Potter, for example. I could do twenty different portraits of David Bowie. That's why stories are important: if you don't tell the full story, you can be misunderstood.

My project *Urban Faces* (opposite) was done in 2009 with Polaroid, which brought out a new camera and commissioned ten artists to play with it. I made cut-outs of faces and walked around London finding the features to fill them. I tend to see faces in the oddest places; I find it adds familiarity to strange surroundings, and it's definitely part of my exploration of character. The most unexpected things came together to form the faces, but I didn't stage anything – not even the black carrier bag that wafted across a parking space just at the right time for me to see and photograph a moustachioed man.

In 2007 I published my first book, *Guess Who?*, a collection of eighty portraits, some of which can also be found in this book. I liked the way the title suggested that the viewer might have to make an effort to work out who was being portrayed, while other faces would instantly identify themselves. This is a large part of my work, and it applies to ideas as well as to faces. *Pretty Ugly* is a collection of portraits from the last fourteen years, published internationally in *The Guardian*, the *New York Times*, *Esquire*, *GQ*, *The Economist*, *Empire* and others. It is probably the only place in the world where you will find Lady Gaga, Stalin, Bowie, Hawking, Batman and Hitler together. Some are fairly simple; others are far more complicated and come with more cultural baggage: Bowie (page 211), Kurt Cobain (page 287) and Shakespeare (page 209), for example. My aim with any portrait is to provoke recognition first and then a deeper appreciation of hidden meaning.

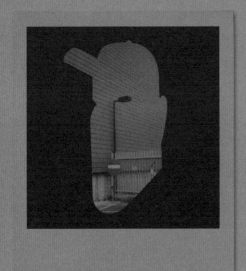

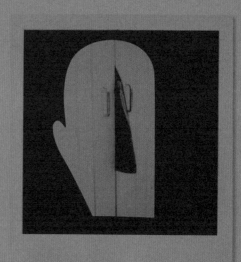

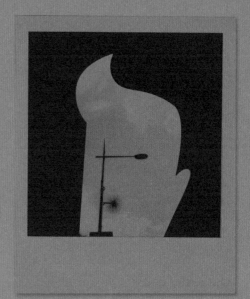
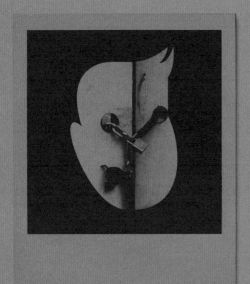

" It all started in Israel, during the first Gulf War, when my country was under missile attack from Iraq. For the first time in my life I had to go into a bomb shelter and wear a gas mask, and while reading the newspaper there, I came across the black radioactivity symbol on its yellow background. As I looked through the blurry visor of my mask, I saw eyebrows and a moustache, and my mind produced the image of Saddam Hussein. I sketched his silhouette around the symbol and all of a sudden it became very much like him. I recreated this image when I moved to London, and sent it out to magazines and newspapers. "

In 2003 people in the editorial world were still sending material by post, still meeting one another, because sending images and portfolios electronically was a new thing and you could never be sure if the person would get it. I left CDs of my work and presented my physical portfolio to lots of editors, including at *Time Out London*. One day I was all packed for a holiday when the art director of *Time Out* rang, asking for a portrait of Shakespeare. I wasn't sure that I could do it, but as I hesitated, the famous line 'To be, or not to be, that is the question' echoed in my mind. This was my personal 'to be, or not to be' moment, and I finished the call with the agreement 'to be'. I sent in my illustration after a few hours; they loved it, and the next day it was on the shelves, exposed to millions of people. It was my first published portrait. "

This portrait was commissioned for an article about a BBC television programme called *The Search for Shakespeare*, which revolved around new biographical discoveries and all the questions they raised. One of the biggest question marks of our existence found a safe home in Shakespeare's face.

The London magazine *Town* requested an image of David Bowie for its Spring 2013 issue, which featured an article about the parts of the city that could be particularly linked with the singer: 'Bowie's London: The Starman of Suburbia'. The article, by curators Geoffrey Marsh and Kathryn Johnson, looked back at his younger days in Brixton, Bromley and Soho as their exhibition 'David Bowie Is' opened at the Victoria and Albert Museum.

One of the twentieth century's most stylish women is represented by the accoutrements of her most famous role, that of Holly Golightly in the film *Breakfast at Tiffany's* (1961). The cigarette-holder, handbag and wide-brimmed hat produce a face that, like Holly herself, is not all it seems.

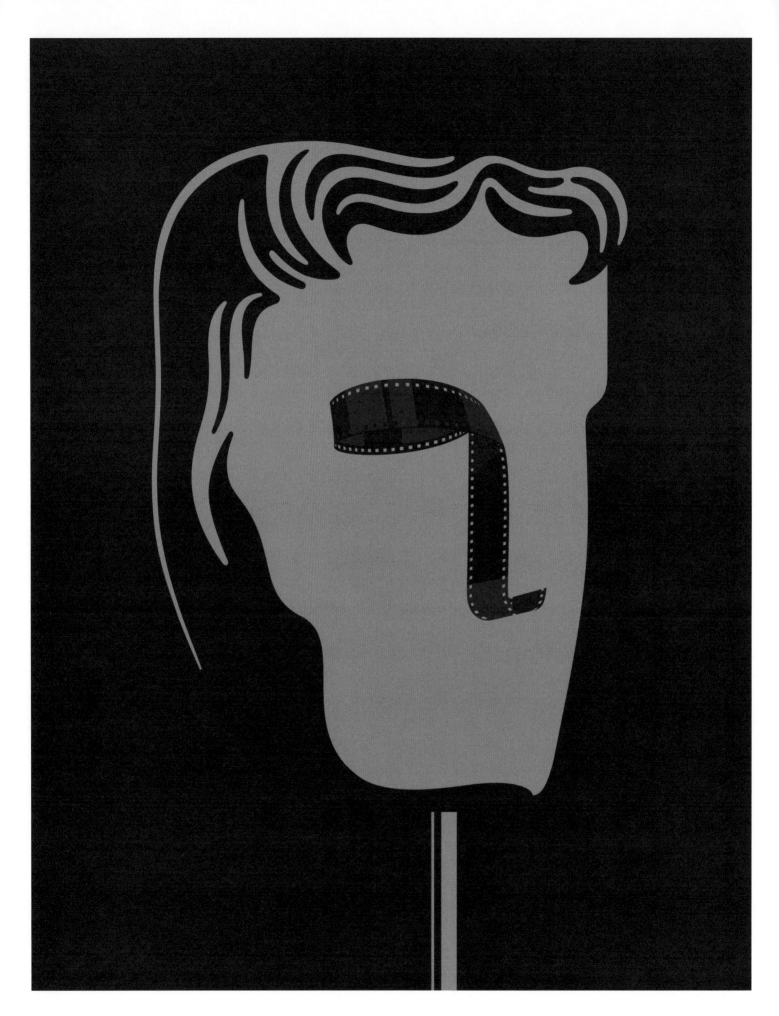

214

66 Working with BAFTA was a unique experience. I had to create the illustrations during judging week, before the winners had been decided. I had a courier at my door twice a day during that week; they would hand me a sealed envelope with a new film for me to watch, and come back to collect it later that day, so I saw all the nominated films without knowing who was going to win. There was an exhibition of all the portraits I had created for the awards ceremony at BAFTA's headquarters on Piccadilly. I also designed the invite for the awards evening, using the famous trophy mask; creating a non-human portrait was a great challenge for me. **99**

Noma illustrated the brochure covers for the BAFTAs in 2009. Each artwork is an interpretation of that year's nominations for best film. Four of the five nominated films are illustrated below (clockwise from top left): *Milk, The Reader, Slumdog Millionaire* and *The Curious Case of Benjamin Button*. Noma was the first illustrator to have his work featured on the brochures.

Basil Fawlty, the henpecked walking disaster brought to life by the actor John Cleese, has become one of the most iconic comedy characters of all time. Combining the angry and disdainful tilt of his distinctive chin with the front desk bell that heralded each new mishap produces an instantly recognizable image. This illustration was commissioned by *UKTV* in August 2005 and reused on the cover of *RIBA Journal* in February 2010.

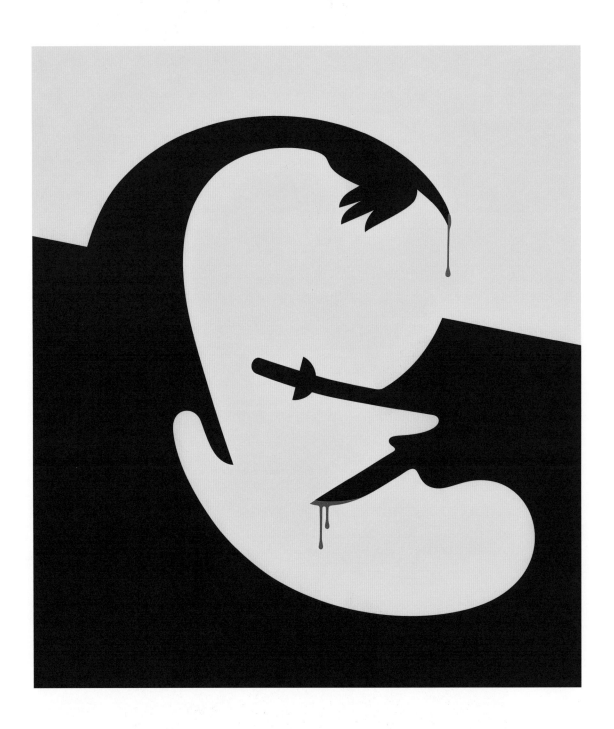

Pulp Fiction, for Empire, May 2014

Pulp Fiction for Gili Chili September 2005

Quentin Tarantino's famously violent film *Pulp Fiction*, starring Uma Thurman, John Travolta and Samuel L. Jackson, came out in 1994. Despite achieving enormous success at the box office, it became thought of as a cult classic; in many ways it redefined the idea itself. The film features a host of colourful characters, including Winston Wolf, the 'clean-up' guy played by Harvey Keitel; Bruce Willis's sour boxer Butch Coolidge; and the mysterious leather-clad Gimp, played by Stephen Hibbert; but the distinctively coiffed tough-guy duo of Travolta and Jackson is an instantly recognizable signifier of the film.

The scowling good looks of Harrison Ford as the womanizing adventurer and archaeologist Indiana Jones, created by George Lucas in homage to the action heroes of the 1930s, are represented here with the curl of a bullwhip and the curve of a bloodstained knife – not to mention the famous (and nine-lived) hat.

»

Noma's images are always distilled, but sometimes a brief requires that he include more elements, as in this image of Steven Spielberg, which reveals more films at each glance. The illustration was done as a section opener for *Empire* on a special box set of Spielberg's top films: *E.T.*, *Jaws* and *Jurassic Park* – the first collection to be approved by the great director himself. A close look at his right eye shows that the hub of the bike's back wheel is not in the centre, but on the right-hand side. This was in fact a mistake – the layer was moved before the illustration went to print – but it is a serendipitous error that captures the slight cast in Spielberg's eye.

Steven Spielberg, for Empire Award, November 2011

Leonard Nimoy, who played Mr Spock in *Star Trek* and devised the 'live long and prosper' salute, mentioned in an interview that he had decided the Vulcans were 'hand-orientated' people, although it is said that several of the actors on *Star Trek* had trouble with the gesture and had to position their fingers off-camera first. This minimal, perfectly balanced image was done for the 'Genius' issue of *Esquire*, but has been republished many times, including on the cover of the *Washington Post* in February 2015, after Nimoy's death.

This instantly recognizable portrait was created using a prop that hints at its subject's profession – a pestle and mortar – while his tongue is represented by a powdery spice. Jamie Oliver's straightforward, cheery persona is reflected in the simple colours and bold shapes. The illustration was made before the chef's rise to prominence with his Fifteen restaurants, Jamie food chain and high-profile campaigns, when he was known primarily for introducing people who thought they couldn't cook to good, basic food.

Jamie Oliver, 1st JULY, 2008

In 2011 a special 'Noma Bar range' of ten classic cult films, each with specially designed sleeve artwork, was brought out by Sony Pictures. The DVDs were issued in a limited edition of just 1,500 copies each.

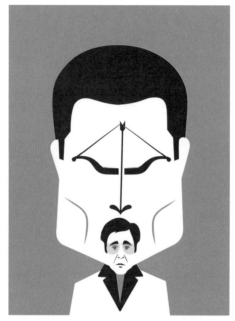
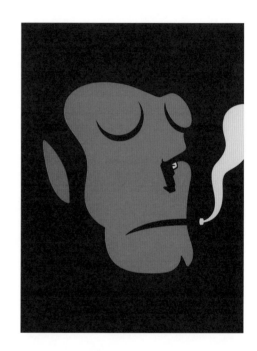

In 2014 a ten-disc collection of Stanley Kubrick's most celebrated films was released, among them *A Clockwork Orange*, *Lolita*, *The Shining* and *Dr Strangelove*. It was featured in *Empire*'s *Re.view* section, for which Noma produced this mash-up cover.

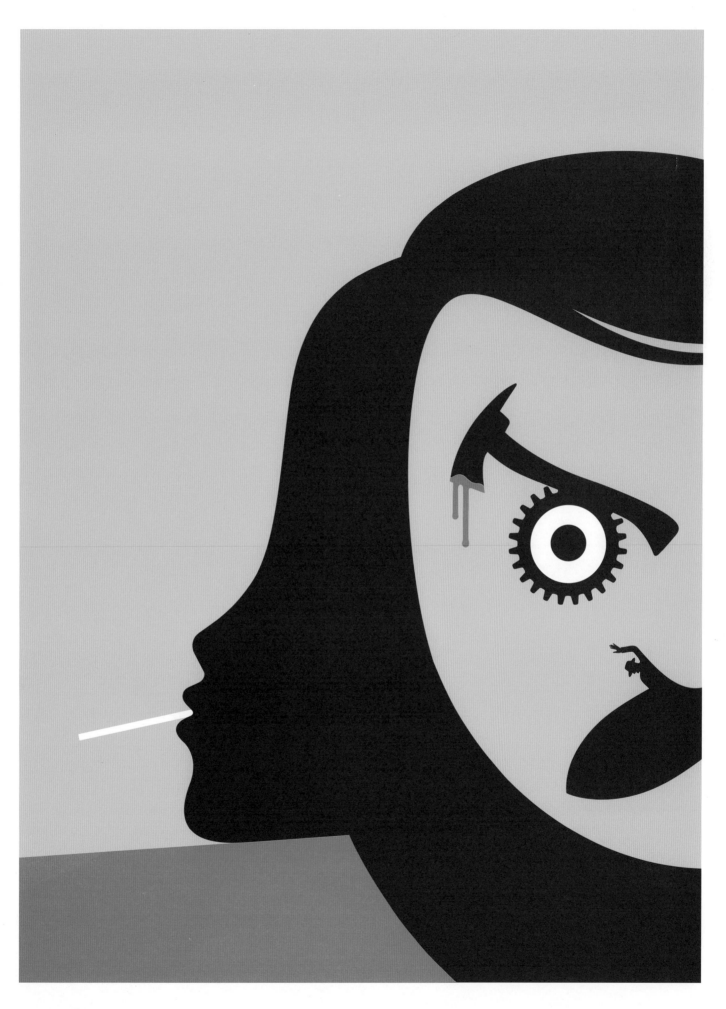

Stanley Kubrick, cover for *Empire Review*, January 2013

Abraham Lincoln, for the *New York Times Book Review*, 4 February 2015

'Abraham Lincoln was the best president the United States has ever had. But we live inside his tomb.' So said the writer of the *New York Times* double book review illustrated by this image. The first assassination of an American president in office shook the country and still resonates today. But perhaps most distinctive about Lincoln, for all his presidential acumen, was the lasting impression of his physical size and the manner of his death. This portrait of the sixteenth president, emancipator of slaves and preserver of the Union, on his deathbed concentrates on the distinctive beard – evoking the gun that was used to kill him – and ever-present top hat.

The killing of Osama bin Laden by United States Navy Seals on 2 May 2011 prompted many magazine covers and newspaper front pages in varying styles. The combination of his distinctive turban and beard with an image of his most notorious act leaves the viewer in no doubt of his identity; but the illustration is neutral, giving an impression of sadness at the state of the world rather than gloating at his downfall. The image was first made in 2001, and appeared with Noma's first editorial interview, for *Blueprint* in 2004; it was republished by the *New York Times* in 2010 before being picked up by *Internazionale*, Italy, in May 2011.

This far from neutral portrait of the forty-third American president, George W. Bush, relies for its effect on one of the more harrowing images of the Iraq War. The photograph on which it is based was taken in 2003 at Abu Ghraib prison in Baghdad, and was important in the debate about whether images showing military abuse of wartime detainees should be released to the public. Noma's illustration places full responsibility for the war on Bush's shoulders.

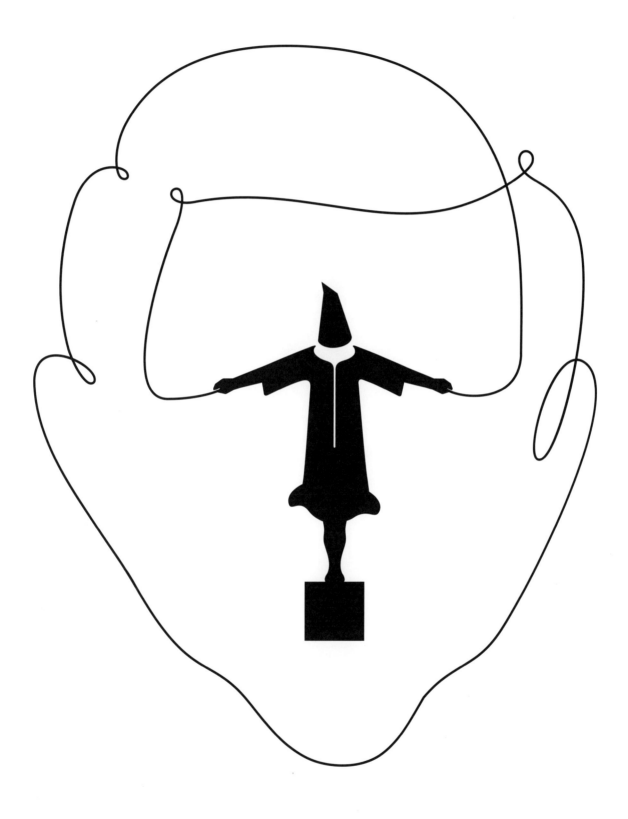

" David Ortiz is a star player who doesn't always behave well, yet is adored by the Red Sox fans. I wanted to portray this dual nature – beloved and controversial – in the illustration opposite. "

The portrait below almost speaks for itself with a slurred 'Adddrrrian'. The boxing gloves give a sense of movement as Rocky takes a one-two punch, but they also form the angular, crumpled features of Sylvester Stallone as he recoils under the blow. Meanwhile, the *Boston Globe* produced an issue that focused entirely on David Ortiz (opposite), a long-time star of the Boston Red Sox baseball team. This engaging yet controversial player was the face of the franchise, and their best power hitter, yet had tested positive for an illegal substance and frequently complained about contracts and scoring decisions. The Ortiz cover was awarded a silver medal by the Society of News Design in 2016.

240

To mark the London Olympics in 2012, the free morning paper *Metro* ran cover wraps featuring celebrated athletes. The Adidas-sponsored covers were part of the 'Take the Stage' campaign, through which they could be taken into any of the sports giant's shops and exchanged for a limited-edition print of the illustration. Noma's subject, the second in the series, was the popular and celebrated cyclist Bradley Wiggins: 'The speedster with sideburns – He's the Mod with the Midas touch who's racing from the Tour to the time trial, where he's looking to turn yellow into gold.'

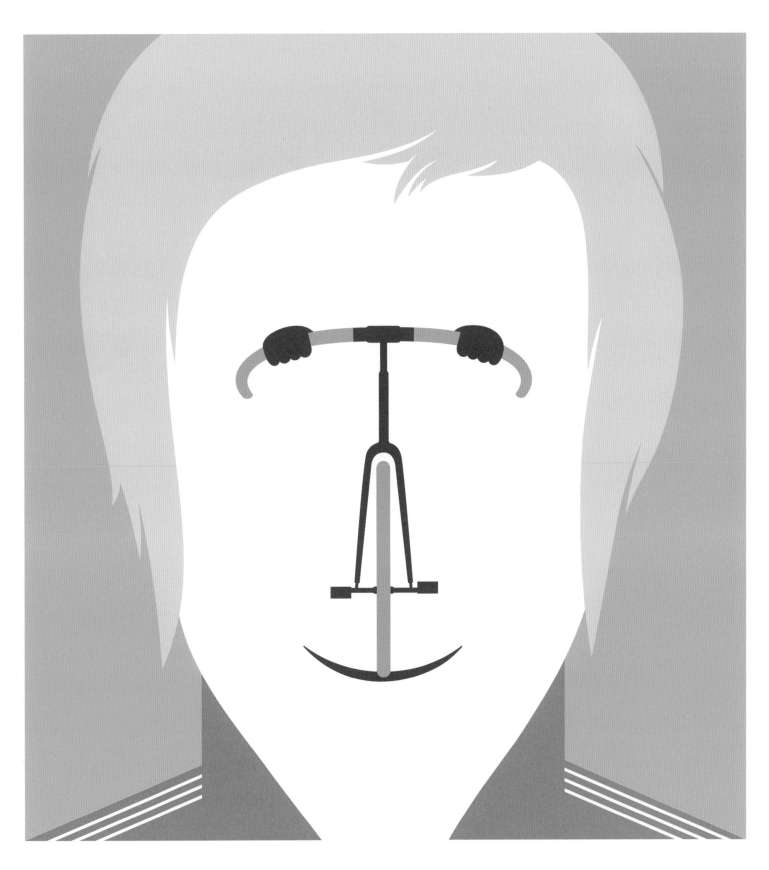

A face that Noma sketched on his laptop (below) led to a portrait of the computing giant Steve Jobs (opposite) for *Wired*. A selection of Jobs's former colleagues and partners, design gurus and commentators offered essays on the inspiring business attitude of the 'defining radical CEO of our era'. The illustration also appeared on the cover of *Internazionale* magazine in October 2011, after Jobs's death.

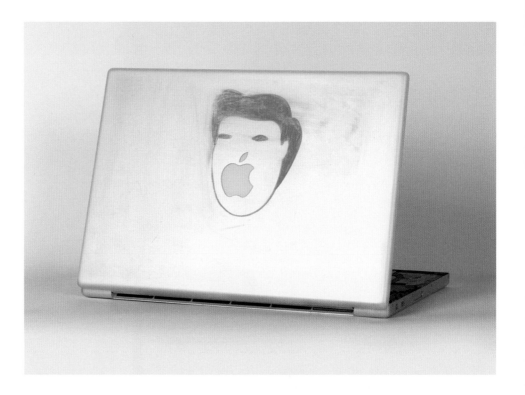

Steve Jobs, for Wired, July 2011

We have all been exposed to the Harry Potter phenomenon. The success of the image below left is in the way it speaks directly of J.K. Rowling's fictional story, as well as the reality of this multimillion-dollar industry. The centrepiece of the illustration is the wand, which evokes fanciful magic, as well as the almighty dollar. On the right, Harry's face is combined with that of his beloved owl Hedwig, and opposite it is formed by quidditch equipment, for an article about that famous invented game.

Harry Potter, for *Time Out London*, July 2011

The distinctive black shapes of the ominous Sith helmets inspired two illustrations on the theme of *Star Wars*. In 2012 a special issue of the free magazine *Shortlist* (opposite) tried to get to the bottom of the enduring popularity of the franchise. An article in *Bloomberg Businessweek* later that year looked at Disney's risk-averse approach to film production in light of its acquisition of Lucasfilm, the company behind the movies, suggesting that while the sale might make more *Star Wars* films possible, it would probably preclude the development of new blockbusters.

Mousetrap, for Bloomberg Businessweek, 8 November 2012

In this portrait of Charlie Chaplin, a famous on-screen moment is used to define the actor's face. Inspired by the shoe-eating scene in the classic silent comedy *The Gold Rush* (1925), in which Chaplin starred, the eye and nose are formed by a shoelace-cum-spaghetti strand, while the shoe doubles as mouth and moustache.

»

Like David Bowie, the cultural icon Bob Dylan is no stranger to interpretation. Here, musical notes, a guitar and a harmonica portray the depth of his influence. Noma's use of an electric guitar, the famous Fender Stratocaster, might be controversial to some aficionados of the singer: when he 'went electric', at the Newport Folk Festival in 1965, many fans accused Dylan of selling out and booed him. He was so angry at this treatment that he refused to return to the festival until 2002. The guitar itself was auctioned for nearly a million dollars in 2013, becoming the most expensive guitar ever to be sold at auction.

This portrait was commissioned to accompany a review of Tina Brown's *The Diana Chronicles* in 2007, published nearly ten years after the princess's death. The book reveals just how powerful, and how marketable, Diana became in the age of modern celebrity-focused journalism, and how she became increasingly expert at manipulating the press – exposure that ultimately contributed to her death.

This article on Darwinism, which appeared just before the 150th anniversary of the publication of *On the Origin of Species*, pointed out that for some people, evolution seems to 'stop at the neck': many believe that our anatomy has evolved, but that our behaviour is culturally determined. It examined our reasons for committing crimes and why it might be difficult for those in positions of power to change our behaviour.

The brief for this illustration of the former British prime minister David Cameron referred to the comic-book hero Plastic Man, created in 1941, whose many superhuman powers include Shape-Shifting, Invulnerability and Regeneration. The man within the face is flexible and ready to squeeze himself out of any tricky situation. The article itself examined Cameron's Christian faith, and the extent to which it was reflected in the priorities shown by his politics.

》

The old Tory logo of a flaming torch is reduced to smouldering embers as it defines Margaret Thatcher's face in this illustration, hinting at the lasting influence of Thatcherism. Its implications for subsequent prime ministers, both Conservative and Labour, were discussed in this article, which examined the Iron Lady's paradoxical personality and what that meant in political terms for a changing country.

When it became clear that the legendary Dutch footballer and coach Johan Cruyff was dying, the editor of *De Volkskrant* asked Noma for a portrait. The image focused on Cruyff's image as a younger man, and expressed certainty that he would occupy a position of honour in the big team in the sky.

The distinctive open countenance and raised eyebrows of the United Nations' eighth Secretary-General, Ban Ki-moon, form a quiet portrait of a quiet man. 'I grew up in war,' says Ban, who is South Korean, 'and saw the United Nations help my country to recover and rebuild. That experience was a big part of what led me to pursue a career in public service. As Secretary-General, I am determined to see this Organization deliver tangible, meaningful results that advance peace, development and human rights.' This article reported on his efforts to solve the crisis in the western region of Sudan in 2007.

This image of Wayne Rooney simultaneously evokes the footballer's face and refers to the subject of the article by Gavin Newsham in British Airways' in-flight magazine. The football encapsulated in the pound sign echoes the concern of many that footballers simply earn more money than is good for them.

»

This article for *Men's Health* magazine looked at the three eras of Schwarzenegger. First was 'body-building Arnie'; second came 'film-star Arnie'; and third was 'statesman Arnie', for which Noma made the illustration opposite. Schwarzenegger followed his huge success in the film industry by turning his attention to politics, and he served as governor of California from 2003 to 2011.

❝ I remember meeting the art director of *GQ* to discuss a portrait of Michael Jackson. The story was about the mothers who had left their children with the singer. I was washing my hands in the bathroom when I glanced at the nappy-changing icon (below) and saw Jackson's face around it: the solution revealed itself. **❞**

Michael Jackson, for GQ, 2005

Brightly coloured flags set off these two portraits, of reggae star Bob Marley, and singer and LGBT rights activist Lady Gaga. The Ethiopian flag seen behind Marley refers to his worship of Haile Selassie, Rastafarianism's Messiah and emperor of Ethiopia between 1930 and 1974. Lady Gaga became an LGBT icon with the release of 'Born This Way' in 2011, and here the rainbow pride flag symbolizes the mixed LGBT community and the hope of a life for all without persecution.

"" Making a portrait of Hitler is an emotional challenge: visually, he is a great character with the iconic toothbrush moustache and uncut hairstyle, but all the time his acts echo in my mind. His regime killed a large part of my family in Europe during the Second World War, and drawing him makes me feel as though I'm humanizing him, even if I'm doing it for an informative article. Over the years, after doing a few portraits of him, I have come to realize the therapeutic side, the fact that it helps me to deal with the trauma. ""

An article in *Esquire* looked at the continuing trend for releasing books about Hitler (nearly 1,000 are listed on Amazon, and at least eleven new titles were published in September 2006 alone), so the choice of barcode as moustache was perfect. The writer examined the apparently endless fascination for the dictator – which seems to be largely a British phenomenon – and concluded that perhaps its power lay in the image of the Second World War as Britain's finest hour, a classic true story of sheer pluck defeating a shocking and powerful regime.

> " I wasn't asked to do a series of straightforward illustrations. We saw an opportunity to tell an imaginative story while staying loyal to each character. This was my own reworking of these famous characters, and I felt that when fans discovered their unique elements, they would feel as though they owned them. "

In 2016 Noma was commissioned by Coca-Cola to produce designs for a limited-edition six-pack of mini-cans featuring Marvel superheroes. Shown opposite, clockwise from top left, are Falcon, Ant-Man, Black Widow and Captain America; Noma also illustrated the Incredible Hulk and Iron Man. The edition of 30,000 was developed with collectors in mind, and carried out in the distinctive Coca-Cola colours.

This portrait of the troubled musician Amy Winehouse was made before her death in 2011, after Noma saw her wandering the streets of Camden, stoned. The famous beehive hair would have been enough to identify her instantly, but the other elements in the illustration give a clue to what eventually caused her downfall.

Mention sex and politics and it is hard not to think immediately of Silvio Berlusconi (opposite), who fell from political grace after accusations of financial irregularity and of having sex with an underage prostitute at one of his infamous 'bunga bunga' parties. This portrait was made not long before he resigned as prime minister of Italy. Elvis (below) is of course an iconic face, and one that has been pictured countless times. The image is made up of three guitars, which combine with an air of cool and the ubiquitous turned-up white collar to produce a portrayal that is full of character.

The forty-fifth American president Donald Trump (below) is a gift to the illustrator, with his trademark hair and exaggerated mannerisms. Barack Obama (opposite), on the other hand, is given a much more dignified portrait that shows his achievement as Nobel Peace Prize laureate and first black president of the United States.

In an article to mark twenty years since Kurt Cobain's suicide – entitled 'Forget the Drugs and the Shotgun: It Was Always About the Music' – *NME* published brand-new personal accounts of the singer by the people he had admired most, including Sonic Youth, the Slits and Iggy Pop. In Noma's portrait, which appeared on the front cover, musical notes and instruments make up the facial features – most notably, perhaps, the singer's signature Fender Jaguar guitar, which forms the beard.

Noma chose to use the dove of peace and a naked olive branch with one last leaf to celebrate the life of Nelson Mandela. Imprisoned for twenty-seven years for his efforts to free South Africa from apartheid, he became a symbol of peace in the struggle for justice and equality, and went on to serve as the country's first black president following his release from prison in 1990.

LIFE

DEATH

I was born in Israel in October 1973, during the tragic Yom Kippur War (the Arab–Israeli War). From the very beginning I lived this bloody war, and my early drawings are full of guns, tanks, helicopters and graphic army symbols. My grandmother lived with us, but I didn't understand why she cried every night in her sleep until I learned at school about the Second World War. She had migrated from Romania to Israel in the 1950s, a widow of forty with a thirteen-year-old daughter and no money, but a great tailoring talent that helped them to survive. Because of her, I was surrounded by craft from an early age: sewing machines, copies of *Burda* magazine and hard-working women in clouds of cheap French perfume.

I decided to apply to my dream college, the Bezalel Academy of Arts and Design in Jerusalem, after a difficult time on national service in the Navy, living away from home in close quarters with strangers, and turning to drawing as a way to regain the individualism that I felt I was in danger of losing. I started to draw my comrades' boots, producing endless drawings in charcoal, pen and ink that went into my portfolio. I don't know exactly why I only drew boots, but it worked, and a few years later the college accepted me. There, I finally found my place and my people – those who make things, who use the creative side of their brain. At Bezalel I studied type design and did projects about the Arab–Israeli conflict. In 1998, when I was in my second year, I got a job making graphics for television news programmes at Channel 2. The style of American television had overtaken the Israeli channels, and every local election had become an animated computer-generated image.

We used to work hard before the morning show, then have breakfast in the kitchen. One day I noticed that all our bendy drinking straws were ordered perfectly on the notice board. I liked it, so I put a long piece of coloured masking tape on the wall behind it. On my next shift, a few days later, a CD had been stuck to the wall. The next day I added a sticker, then a car ad from a magazine appeared. I put up a pen drawing of the room, and the mystery person hung a flashy parrot picture above it. Then the iconography turned, and I found a drawing of a knife; the next day, a handcuffed character, a bleeding Mickey Mouse and a drawing of a mosque. I realized that I was sharing the kitchen walls with a Palestinian. I was keen to know who he or she was, but the few Palestinian reporters at Channel 2 denied all knowledge of the artwork. The last option was Nimmer, a quiet Palestinian cleaner who worked nights. One morning I came in to do my shift before college and it was all gone. A sign from the management on the newly cleared walls said simply that our display was ugly and had been removed. I came back in the evening to catch Nimmer and ask if it had been him, but he wasn't working that shift, or the next. It turned out that he had been dismissed for allegedly looking at the journalists' mail and documents.

Encounters like this have made me want to create more unusual connections and dialogues, and not to shy away from difficult political subjects. They have also motivated me to undertake projects like 'Cut the Conflict' (see pages 382–95), in which I juxtaposed material sent to me by people in warring countries, allowing those individuals to communicate and collaborate in a way that they otherwise couldn't. I'm not a politician or a soldier, but a lot of people see my artworks, and through them I would like to be able to change how we deal with political problems, and what we think about the nations with which our own countries may disagree. The influences of my background make me well suited to these subjects. The experience you gain between the ages of eighteen and twenty-one has a huge effect on the rest of your life, and at that age I was doing my national service in the Navy. I feel as though I have knowledge of things that most illustrators don't have.

A lot of my editorial work is for the 'opinion' section of *The Guardian*. It has to be done quickly: the text of the article will arrive at lunchtime and the illustration must be ready by 6 p.m., and during the afternoon the copy can change if the news changes. First I must get to the point of the 300-word article so that I can make a good illustration, and then I'm talking to the editor constantly, receiving immediate feedback. It is printed the next day, and I am exhausted afterwards. It's satisfying and I love it, but it's not a relaxed way of working, as other briefs are. My favourite part of the process is the joy of seeing my work come out. After an intimate process, in which I draw in my sketchbook and finesse the piece in my studio, suddenly 13 million people see it in the paper and online. I never get used to that. The next day I will go to my local shop and buy the paper, show my illustration to the newsagent owner and talk it over with him. It's a bit of a ritual.

Working with the words of an article, I always try to say more than one thing at a time. With my illustration of the Statue of Liberty for *Aeon* (page 344), for example, the reader will see the gun, then read the article, look again and see the crying person. People generally aren't looking for additional meanings, so when they see that extra thing they're pleased, as though they're in on a secret. They even want to tell others. It gives a personalized twist to the work, because what looks like an ordinary illustration is out of the ordinary when you look again. My aim as I strip down my sketched ideas is to produce a modest-looking image that hides something. I want to make it simple, so that it's not hard to discover the hidden element and the reader can focus on the story.

The story can be social as well as political, or focus on money, religion, healthcare, the environment . . . *Life Death* is a varied collection of positive observations on the negativity in our lives. My work for newspapers and magazines has meant that I've dealt with a lot of difficult subjects, but many contain at least a grain of positivity if you can just find it – whether it's people pulling together in the aftermath of a terrorist attack, an unexpected scientific finding that offers hope to those suffering from a medical condition, or news of a charity or government standing up for an oppressed group of people. With my work on these topics, I try to let the reader step away from the emotiveness of the subject without ignoring it altogether. I also try to link the puzzle of my illustrations with the idea that a larger problem needs to be solved. Ultimately, my goal with difficult topics is to make them easier to understand, and at the same time underline their importance.

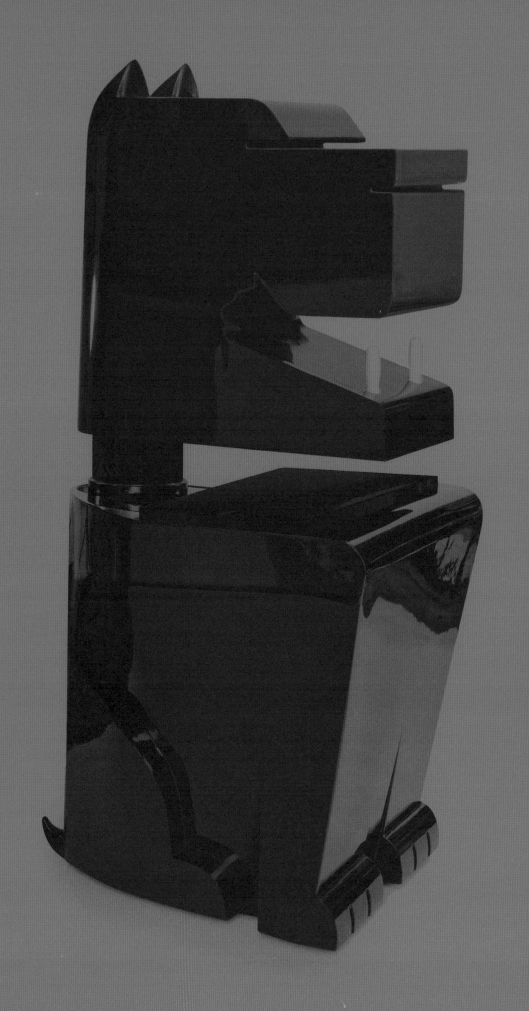

It's Nice That approached me to design covers for reissues of thirteen novels by Don DeLillo, a summary of more than thirty years of his writing. I started to pull out some of the main elements of each story and tried to understand how DeLillo had tailored them. The result is a bold image for each cover that looks conventional at first, but at a second glance reveals the whole story.

The London-based creative agency It's Nice That art-directed a set of new editions of the works of the American writer Don DeLillo, and enlisted Noma to produce the cover designs. It's Nice That commented: 'It seemed obvious that the subtlety and craft in Noma's work was the perfect vehicle to try and communicate DeLillo's intricate and often sinister subjects . . . the DeLillo reissues could not have fit more perfectly.' The series won a D&AD Yellow Pencil in 2012.

On 7 January 2015 the offices of the French satirical magazine *Charlie Hebdo* were attacked by Islamist terrorists, killing ten journalists – including much-loved cartoonists – and two police officers. The pen and pencil quickly became icons in the international response to the shocking attack.

The Israel–Palestine Peace Conference brings together Israeli and Palestinian decision-makers, writers and philosophers with world leaders. Noma was asked to create a cover and a poster for the conference, and used the biblical idea of the wolf living with the lamb to produce an image that can be read from either side. Among the contributors to the conference in 2014 were Barack Obama, Ban Ki-moon and Tony Blair.

Paris Attacks, cover for De Volkskrant, Netherlands, 16 November 2015

On 13 November 2015 the so-called Islamic State orchestrated attacks
on five locations in Paris, killing 130 people and leaving many more
injured. It was one more atrocity in a shocking sequence of such attacks
in France.

The Italian magazine *Internazionale* offers articles from around the world translated into Italian. After the terrorist attacks in Paris on 13 November 2015, it produced a special supplement illustrating the front covers created worldwide in response to the tragedy. Noma's illustration was chosen for the front cover.

The distinctive Twitter and Facebook icons are subverted here for two pieces about social media. In 2013, a few months before she died, Peaches Geldof provoked a criminal investigation when she identified on Twitter two parents who had allegedly allowed their two children to be sexually abused. Her actions effectively identified the children themselves to her huge number of followers. Meanwhile, in America, details of an alleged rape came out through posts made by the perpetrators on social media, despite the fact that the apparent victim had no memory of the crime.

The Face of Crime, for the New Yorker, 5 August 2013

This page and opposite and opposite: Covers in Elphonot, Science Issue, February 2012

66 This idea turned up one night in the small hours, a few weeks before my solo exhibition in Paris. I was casting about for a 3D piece for a corner of the gallery, but nothing was happening – I was too tired. Suddenly an ink drip in my sketchbook looked like a burnt-out match that formed my profile, perfectly expressing my feelings in those busy, stressful weeks. 99

Positive News is a magazine, published online and in print, that is committed to high-quality, inspiring journalism, focusing on the possibility for progress rather than reporting on disaster and hardship. For an article on how domestic workers around the world were coming together to fight for better conditions, Noma integrated human faces into common household objects to shine a spotlight on their efforts to be heard.

Rape, which has long been a spoil of war, is an under-reported but widespread tool of humiliation and terror, and has also been used strategically. In this illustration, fighter jets streak over a desert that deserves a second look.

In 2014 Noma worked with Greenpeace UK on a campaign to highlight the importance of small-scale fishermen to Britain's coastal communities and healthy coastal ecosystems, and the threat posed to them by large-scale foreign 'monster boats'. The fish cunningly hidden in the depiction of David and Goliath vessels reminds us of the riches of our oceans.

A debate about the pressure faced by children prompted this article in *The Guardian* on the weak and even scornful response of liberals – afraid of expressing any preference for the past in case it brings accusations of conservatism – to the problem of improving children's well-being. The writer finished with a stark warning: 'Progressive politics has to put the interests of human beings ahead of the demands of business. Its role must be to analyse and act on the patterns of behaviour the market and contemporary culture are imposing on us. To accept instead without question would be the truly conservative act.' Noma used an image of the hoodie-wearer, a vilified group in 2000s Britain and symbolic of the unhappy and discontented teenager, but is the match illuminating or igniting the problem?

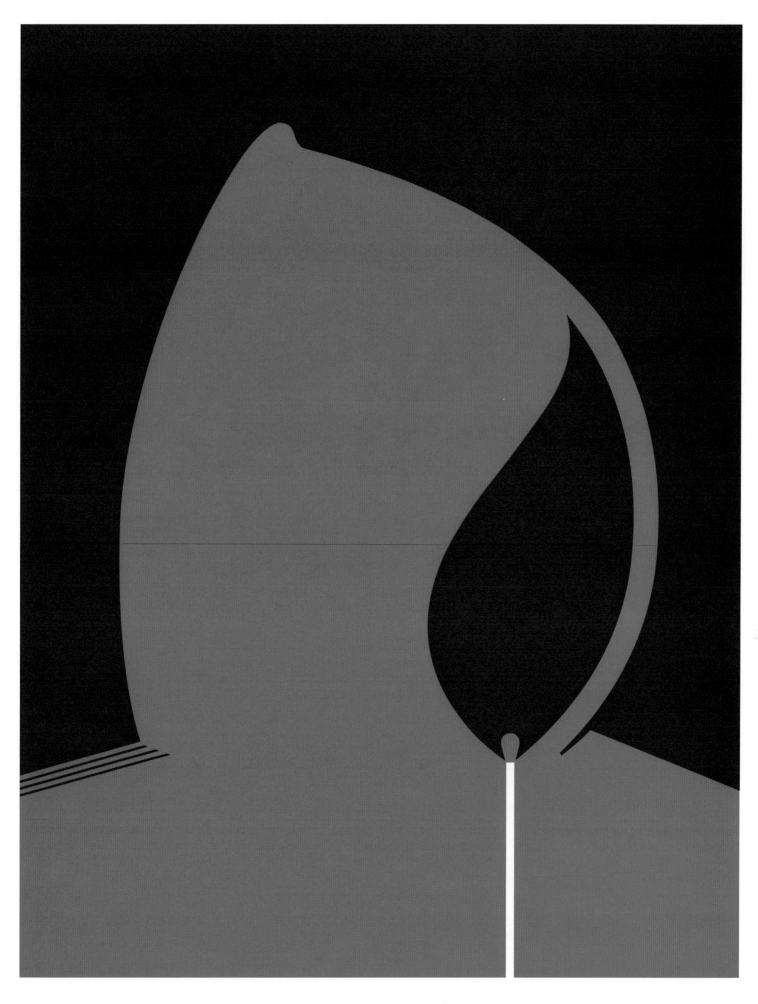

Before the UK general election in 2010, the anti-fascist organization EMMA (Ethnic Multicultural Media Academy) mounted a campaign online and in print. Using graphic, provocative images associated with Nazism, it urged members of the public to acknowledge the importance of using their democratic voice to stand up against the far-right British National Party. This campaign was also the first time that a graphic poster had been projected onto the Houses of Parliament in London. The campaign was nominated for a D&AD award.

Illustration for Greenpeace Magazin, Peace Issue, Germany, January/February 2016

Zwarte Piet, or Black Peter, is a traditional Dutch character who is the companion of the better-known St Nicholas (Sinterklaas, from whom the American Santa Claus originated). Piet is a black man who punishes naughty children; among many theories about his folkloric origin are suggestions that he was a black slave who was freed by Nicholas, or that he is not in fact black but merely a chimney sweep who is covered in soot. Whatever its history, the continued evocation of this figure has in recent years been criticized and campaigned against as racist and outdated. It is defended by many Dutch people, some of whom still wear costumes and black make-up to portray the character. In a country that is renowned worldwide for its liberal, tolerant culture, Black Peter is a tradition that is widely considered unacceptable.

Cover for *Vrij Nederland*, Netherlands, 23 November 2014

The doves' heads fold nicely into the Volkswagen camper, mourning the loss of the hippy dream. This image was produced as a possible cover for Gerard DeGroot's *The Sixties Unplugged*, but in the end was placed on the back. *When Doves Cry* has since become a popular screenprint.

Malaria still kills three million people a year, and prevention efforts have shifted in focus from eradication to personal protection. The disease is most rampant in Africa, where new mosquito-net technology promises a breakthrough. The Japanese pharmaceutical company Sumitomo has engineered long-life extruded-resin nets that secrete repellent, with the potential of ending malaria as the world knows it. Noma's illustration for this article by Jon Snow reminds us of the threat posed by the disease.

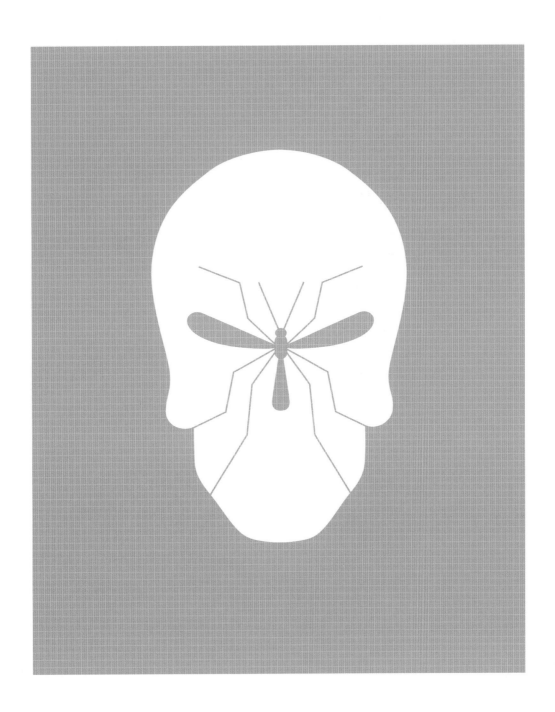

In 2011 Noma created a series of monochrome illustrations with the advertising agency BBH to promote *Injustice*, a five-part drama on ITV1 about a barrister who has lost faith in the legal system but becomes involved in a new case.

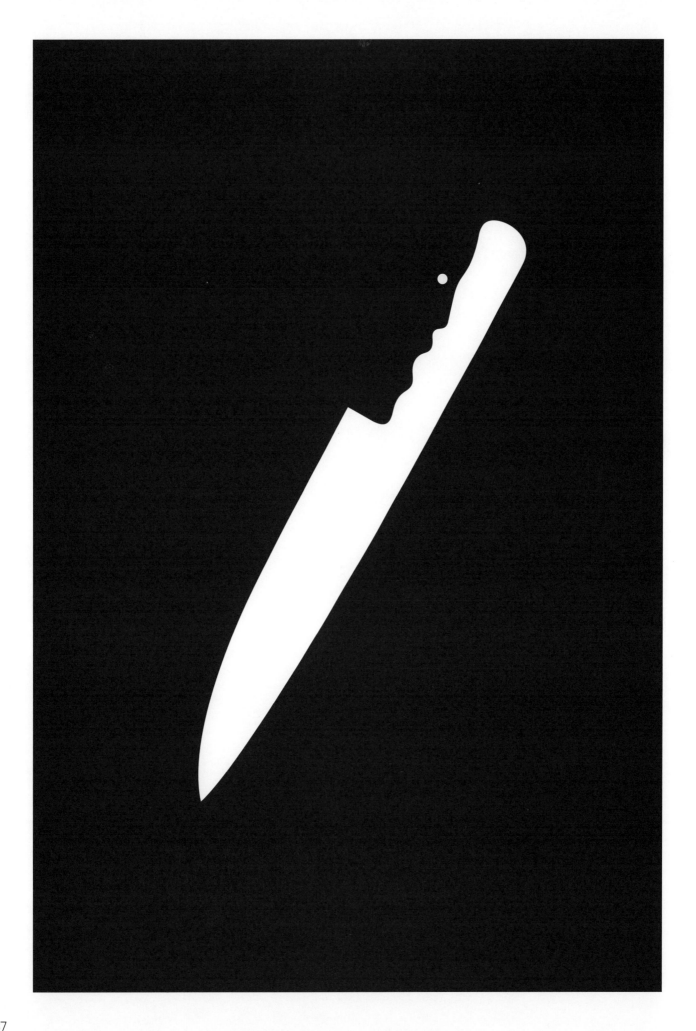

The illustration below provided a stark reminder of the human toll of drug-trafficking, as dealt with in wide-ranging and startling detail in Roberto Saviano's book *ZeroZeroZero*, reviewed in this article by Mark Bowden. The depiction of drug-taking is neither common nor accepted in mainstream culture, but this illustration, with its double meaning, runs no risk of glamorizing the practice.

»

In 2013 *Time Out London* ran a comprehensive survey of drug-taking in the capital – a trend-leader for new substances, 'if not as high as it was in the late '90s and early noughties' – to investigate what was being taken, where and by whom. Cannabis was the most widely taken drug, with 90 per cent of respondents saying they had used it. Also among the survey's findings were the strange substances that Londoners have used to try to get high, such as nutmeg ('It was pre-internet'), the painkiller Nurofen ('That was stupid, not weird') and hash yoghurt.

Cover for *Time Out London*, Drugs Issue, 19–25 February 2013

Gun Crime cover for *Internazionale*, Italy, 29 June–5 July 2012

The illustration opposite accompanied a report in *Internazionale* magazine from Ciudad Juárez in Mexico, a symbol of a country besieged by drug traffickers and an important front in the battle for the new president. The general election was eventually won by Enrique Peña Nieto. The illustration below was done for an article about the constant battle against shoplifters waged by British shops. 'It's a war of attrition,' said one commentator – a war that store detectives, assistants and security companies, despite their constant vigilance, are not winning. Although not used in the newspaper, the image became a print and a wooden cut-out.

On 3 July 1981 the *New York Times* reported on a rare form of 'cancer' that appeared to be affecting only gay men: 'Eight of the victims died less than 24 months after the diagnosis was made,' it reported. No one at the time grasped the full horror of the situation, and thirty years later *Washingtonian* reflected on the course of the AIDS epidemic and the lives it changed, through the voices of those in the city who experienced it in some way.

«

The gun lobby in the United States claims that guns keep us safe from criminals; this article investigated the opinion of social scientists, who broadly agree that the idea that 'guns save lives' is profoundly untrue. In this illustration the Statue of Liberty raises her gun as two sad faces look on.

Noma has worked with *Internazionale* magazine for many years, in many cases providing a published image for reuse, but sometimes creating a bespoke illustration. In March 2014, in the wake of the Crimean Revolution and Russia's annexation of Crimea, *Internazionale* produced an issue on Crimea's 'Cold War'; and in January 2016 an issue on the tension between Saudi Arabia and Iran prompted the bloodthirsty cover illustration opposite.

In an essay in memory of the Australian journalist Pamela Bone (1940–2008), the writer and broadcaster Clive James asked why more feminists in the West had not spoken out against the treatment of women in Islam. Bone had felt that many Western liberal societies believed non-Western cultures could be only victims, never criminals, 'no matter what atrocities they might condone even within their own families', and James suggested that Western female thinkers were protesting less about honour crimes as the news about them increased. He concluded that men who perpetrated so-called honour killings against women must be roundly condemned as 'the homicidal maniacs they are'. This simple but deeply suggestive image accompanied the article.

So-called content marketing – or brand journalism – is a broad genre that eludes definition, but it essentially involves the creation of journalistic material by brands. It may well be taking over from the traditional, and more overt, direct advertising, and that has implications not only for publishers' advertising revenues but also for the general public, who cannot always be sure whether they are reading an independent piece or a focused, brand-created article. This image of a wolf in sheep's clothing portrays the innocent and unaware public as an easy victim for those with money to make.

In this magazine cover the negative space of the Turkish national flag becomes a direct reflection of the explosive situation there, after civil unrest spread throughout the country in May 2013.

During the week of the European referendum *The Guardian* asked me to prepare two illustrations for its Saturday issue, in the event of a Brexit win. Like many people on both sides, I thought it was pretty unlikely that the UK would vote to leave. When I woke up to the result, I was shocked and upset. I have never before worked on an illustration and hoped so fervently that it wouldn't be used. I imagine the writer of the article felt much the same way as he produced his piece, 'A Farewell to Europe'.

The close vote by British citizens on 23 June 2016 to leave the European Union was a moment of profound shock to many, on both sides of the campaign, and those feelings intensified over subsequent days as many prominent members of the government resigned from public office. The teardrop in the illustration opposite encapsulated the reaction of a left-leaning paper that in the days before the vote had exhorted its readers to vote 'Remain'. In 2017 the cover won the Society for News Design's 'Award of Excellence'.

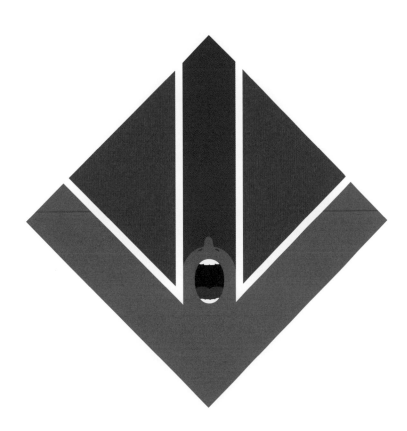

For an article in *Esquire* on how CEOs invest their own wealth, Noma drew the symbol for sterling chomping on a large cigar (below). It was reused by *Internazionale* magazine in April 2011. The illustration opposite accompanied an article about the business practices of Sir Philip Green and the scandal over his role in the collapse of British Home Stores in 2016.

An article by Naomi Klein in *The Guardian*'s *Weekend* section looked at what she called 'on-again-off-again ecological amnesia', in which even those who would consider themselves to be well-informed and environmentally conscientious prioritize their lifestyle over what needs to be done to combat climate change. She argued that the problem lies in the fact that the things we need to do to cut emissions are directly in conflict with the goals of deregulated capitalism, and threaten 'an elite minority with a stranglehold over our economy, political process and media'.

Sticky Business, for Guardian Weekend, 13 September 2014

Stills from Unmasking a Killer, NewYork Productions 2016

Focusing on immunotherapy, *Unmasking a Killer* was the first in a series of short films to help the general public understand the development of new therapies in medicine. The film was first broadcast at the Super Bowl and seen by some 30 million people. It has received accolades from around the world, including an award for film craft at the New York Festivals and two golden Clios. It is now part of the permanent collection of the Museum of Modern Art, New York.

≫

Noma's animation style starts with great images, but that is not enough – each must evolve from the previous scene and lead seamlessly to the next. For the International Day of Peace on 21 September 2015, Noma directed the film *Symbols* for the World Food Programme with TBWA\Chiat\Day New York, voiced by Liam Neeson.

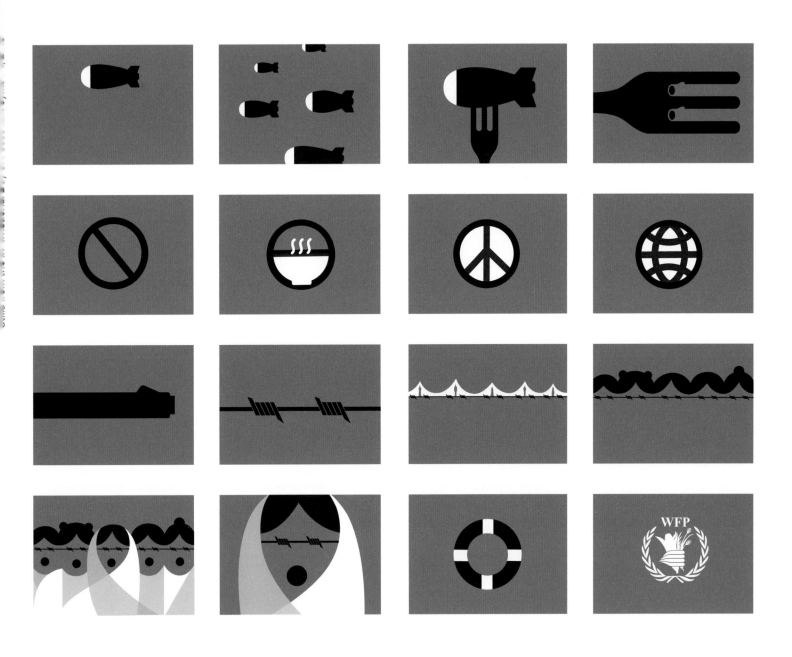

In a week when the ninety-three-year-old 'bookkeeper of Auschwitz' went on trial for being an accessory to more than 300,000 murders, the image of the pen came into play to accompany an article by the historian Richard Evans about how the Nazis' crimes continue to haunt us. As well as the occasional trial for alleged war crimes, the shadow of Nazism falls across fiction, with such films as Tarantino's *Inglourious Basterds* and Polanski's *The Pianist* and such novels as Schlink's *The Reader* and Boyne's *The Boy in the Striped Pyjamas*. As Evans put it, 'the Nazis came to power in a modern European society, a society of great cities, classic buildings, bustling urban streets; economically advanced, technologically sophisticated and culturally literate ... The Nazis and those who served them were wedded to modern technology, racing cars, motorways, cinema, TV, rockets, jet-propelled planes' – and that is something we should remember as the rise of far-right political groups is once more a reality.

Nazi Obsession, for The Guardian, 01 February 2016

In 2015 the airline Emirates showed its support for the animal charity United for Wildlife by decorating two of its A380 jets with images of endangered species. It also ran related stories in its in-flight magazine, *Open Skies*, beginning with a cover story in October about how illegal poaching was affecting rhinos and elephants.

»

As part of the initiative 'Bear in Mind', the start-up consultancy White Bear Studio organized an exhibition and sale in support of the World Wide Fund for Nature. It was held in December 2015 in London and Dublin. Noma's contribution was a polar bear print.

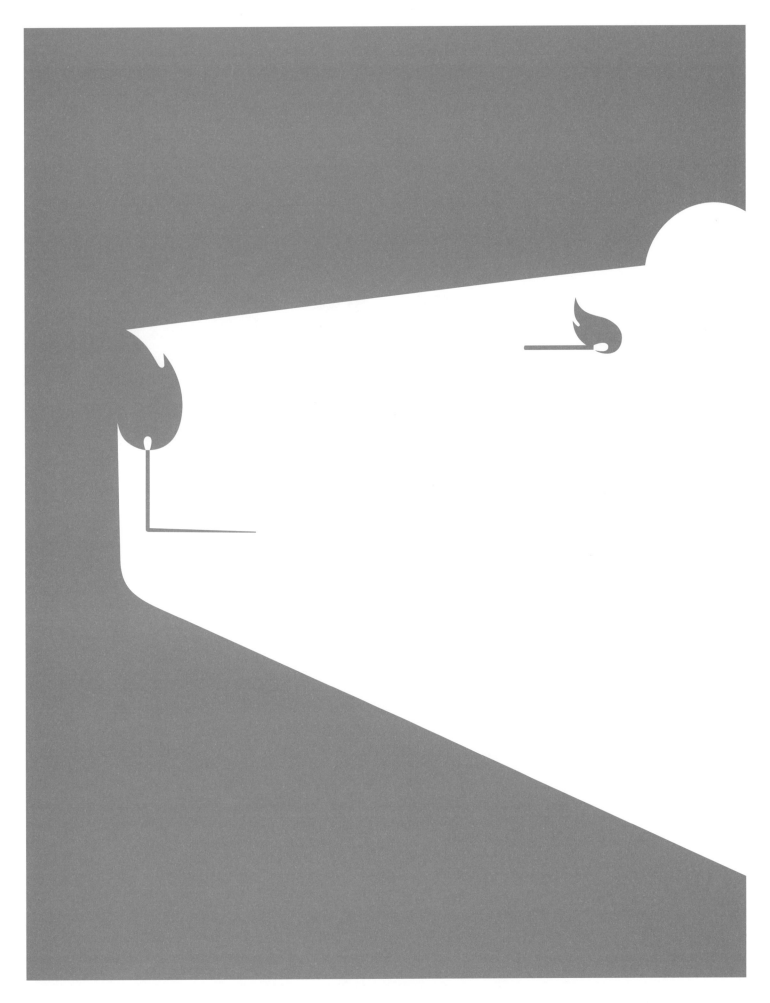

The writer and analyst Aaron David Miller suggested that it was time for the American public to lower its expectations: 'Maybe then we can allow our presidents to be good without expecting them to be great.' Noma's illustration took up the concept of presidential hopefuls being swallowed up by the idea of their predecessors.

»

Noma created a flower-power gun for a prescient article about the limitations of soft power, written a few days after Barack Obama's election to the American presidency. The writer asked how idealism could weather global economic, political and military tumult, and concluded that – despite Obama's charisma and international popularity and the optimism created by his election – great nations 'cannot survive on soft power alone'.

In 2013 *The Guardian*'s US edition launched its first advertising campaign in the United States, with the agency BBH New York. Noma's illustrations were used to depict both sides of an important political debate in the country: individual freedom versus government regulation. Women in the military (opposite, left) and internet privacy/terrorism (opposite, right) were two of the subjects covered with striking posters that could be viewed either way up.

This image underlines the inconsistency of our online behaviour: we share photographs and private information online, but complain about the National Security Agency and other security services spying on us. It seems as though we really do want to have it both ways.

This illustration was made for an article that examined the consequences of human attempts to alter the temperature of the Earth. It took as its starting point the eruption in April 1991 of Mount Pinatubo in the Philippines, which caused global temperatures to fall by nearly 0.5°C. The catastrophe gave geophysical scientists an understanding of what might happen if we tried to achieve a similar result.

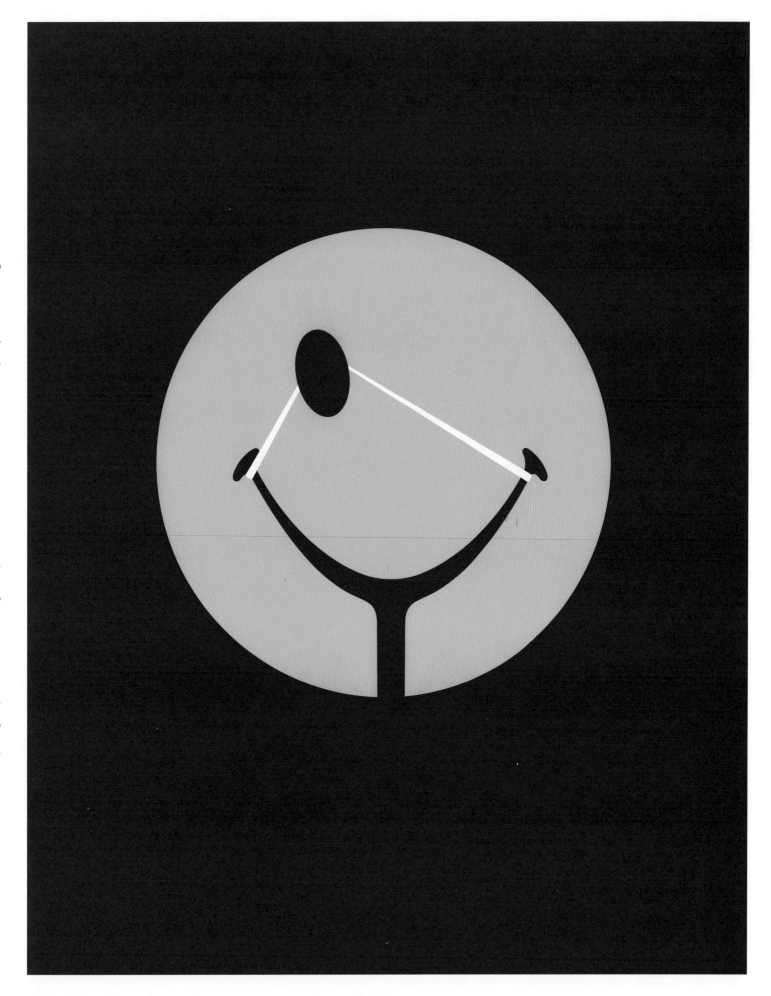

In the wake of child-abuse scandals involving the Catholic Church, the journalist Simon Jenkins suggested that other institutions in the United Kingdom – among them the NHS, the Army and the police force – seemed oddly unconcerned about how their internal procedures were viewed by the general public. The pope's hat here becomes a locked door in a well-defended wall.

»

As her term as president of the British Humanist Association neared its end, the journalist Polly Toynbee offered some thoughts for her successor, the physicist and broadcaster Jim Al-Khalili. She advocated for the question of religion in the national census to be more clearly phrased to give a better picture of religious belief – and lack of it – across the UK; maintained that the 'most urgent' battle concerned the right to die; and argued that humans are born with an innate moral sense that does not require the aid of religious belief.

Noma was commissioned by the refuge organization Harmony House in China to produce images for posters to raise awareness of domestic violence and encourage people to 'see it – don't ignore it'.

An article by a Labour minister insisted that a return to Old Labour after Tony Blair was not a danger, but that a moral goal must be identified. Freedom and the power to use that freedom, he suggested, could be that goal. Meanwhile, the Partnership at Drugfree.org (now the Partnership for Drug-free Kids) commissioned the image opposite for a poster campaign intended to underline its mantra, 'You are not alone', and to help worried parents feel empowered.

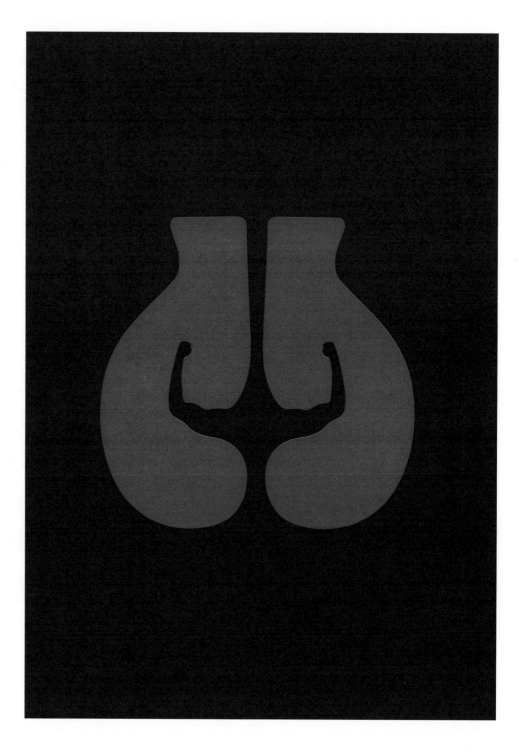

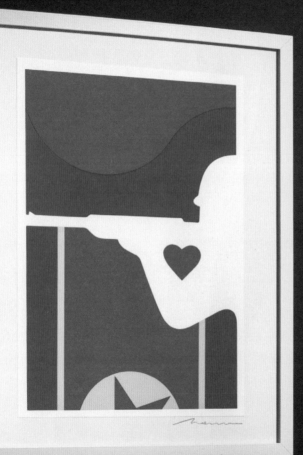

Cut the Conflict

In 2011 Noma unveiled his interactive 'Cut It Out' image-making machine at the London Design Festival, allowing large numbers of his silhouette images to be produced for exhibition-goers. The 2-m-high electric 'dog' began as a virtual three-dimensional model designed by Noma in the shape of one of his best-known illustrations, *S.M.L.*, of a dog, a cat and a mouse. Visitors to the festival could feed the dog with sheets of rubber, paper and other materials and cut them into various designs (there were ten to choose from), which Noma signed and numbered. The idea of Noma's art continuing without him was central to the project, and the cut-outs that visitors produced were all individual. In this way Noma took a new approach to print production, which is usually restricted to signed and numbered limited editions that are created with ink. The project was shortlisted by the Design Museum in London for its 'Designs of the Year' in 2012.

In 2013 Noma brought the machine out again for a show on a subject very close to his heart: the prevalence of conflict across the globe and efforts of all kinds to decrease it. The exhibition, at Rook & Raven Gallery in central London, allowed him to explore the concept of war and peace with the help of the public. The idea came to him when he talked to an Iranian man who lived in London, and realized that such a conversation could never have taken place in either of their home countries. Several months before the start of the show, via his Facebook page, he asked people from countries that were suffering conflict of any kind to send materials to him by post:

Are you from / living in a country in conflict?

If so, I would love you to take part in my upcoming exhibition . . . Please send me materials . . . that represent your country: tapestries, maps, flags, letters, photos, newspapers, packaging, drawings, fabrics, posters, etc.

Following a selection of samples from both sides of a respective dispute, I will create a series of bespoke art works by cutting the materials and mounting them on the same page, forcing them to co-exist peacefully alongside each other forever.

He received an astonishing, almost overwhelming, number of contributions, which he made into graphic cut-out images, each of which contained material from two countries that were in conflict.

The provocation of such images rests in the fact that they allow indirect dialogue between people who, because of the situations of their respective countries, might not otherwise be able or allowed to communicate.

In all the images, a motif of peace is created from a symbol of war: the face of a helmeted soldier becomes a dove, for example; the arm of a man aiming a rifle forms a heart shape; and the simple outline of a handgun, at second glance, becomes that of a bird in flight. The compositions are rendered particularly beautiful through the use of patterned, textured and boldly coloured materials. The contributors were all credited in the final artworks and exhibition.

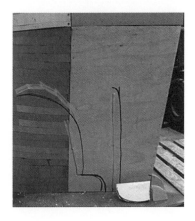

66 For people in some countries, sending materials to a project like this is a risky thing. By submitting such materials, people were demonstrating that they were willing to take a risk, in order to contribute and put their name to my peace project. What I really wanted to achieve was a series of metaphorical handshakes between conflicted countries, to show that dialogue can happen, that there's hope beyond conflict. **99**

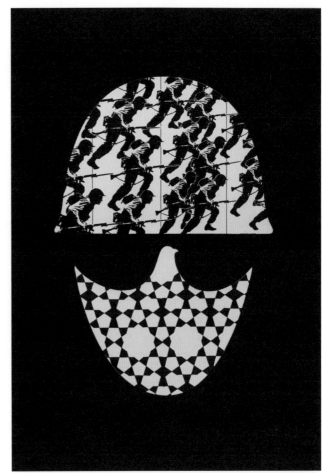

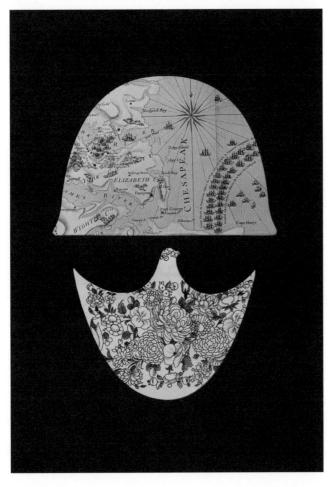

Peace Talks (India/Pakistan), mixed media, from 'Cut the Conflict', 2013

66 I created a map of conflicts and piled up materials from the affected countries. When I paired them, I realized how similar some of the materials were, in texture, subject, etc. For example, the top half of the image opposite is from the Lebanese newspaper *An-Nahar*, and the bottom half is from the Israeli newspaper *Haaretz*. In the image two languages from countries with a long history of war are brought together in harmony. **99**

Make the Right Choice (Lebanon/Israel), mixed media, from 'Cut the Conflict', 2013

Index

Page numbers in *italic* refer to illustrations.

Acknowledgments

Dana – thank you for your friendship, patience, help and support through the long days and white nights. I love you.

My agents and producers Helen Cowley and the Dutch Uncle family in London and New York, Dan Chrichlow, Joel Minter and Mikiharu Yabe (Agent Hamyak in Japan) deserve a special mention. Thank you for all your help.

Deep thanks also go to my parents Zeev Bar (RIP) and Batia Bar, and my sisters Hanita Weiss and Revital Lessick.

Thank you to Lucas Dietrich, Rosie Fairhead, Paul Hammond, Rebecca Pearson and the team at Thames & Hudson, and to Fernando Gutiérrez, Nick Cook and Sam Brogan at Studio Fernando Gutiérrez.

I would like to express my gratitude to the following organizations and individuals:

&&& (Simon Brown); 2D:3D (Rob Edkins and the team); Toni Abi Ad, Arik Prussak and everyone who contributed to 'Cut the Conflict'; Alejo Accini; Adam & Eve/DDB (Charmaine Balay); *Aeon* (Andy Sansom); AGDA (Australian Graphic Design Association); Air Berlin (Stefanie Zimmermann, Meike van Meegen, Anna Rudolf); Ando Foundation (Kenji Koizum, Naomi Katsuyama, Yuji Nakayama, Koichi Hara); *Arise* (Graham Smith); Assimil (Nicolas Ragonneau); BAFTA (Studio Small); Bain & Company (Richard Keenan and Dianne Bain); Algy Batten; BBH London (Sally Green, Nick Kidney, David Kolbusz, Nick Gill, Emmanuel Saint M'Leux, Simon Pearse); BBH New York (Caprice Yu, Devon Hong, Matt Clark, Deb Spokony); Bear Studio (Kelly Mackenzie); Bloomberg (Richard Turley); *Bloomberg Businessweek* (Chandra Illick); *Blueprint* (Patrick Myles); *The Boston Globe* (Joseph Moore); *Business Life* (Belinda Tighe); Channel 4 (Edward Webster); *Chineasy* (ShaoLan, Crispin Jameson, Carissa Chan, Darren Perry and the Thames & Hudson team); Coca-Cola (James Sommerville, Craig E. Stroud, Frederic Kahn, Keisha Curtis); Condé Nast (Bele Engels); *Courrier International* (Luc Briand); *Cycling Plus* (Ben Foxall); D8/Greenpeace (Adrian Carroll, Anna McManus, David Shanks, Jo Stein); The Design Museum, London; *Diplomat* (Jeannine Saba); Dragon Rouge (Lynne Dobney); *The Economist* (Suzy Connolly, Una Corrigan, Sue Vago); *Emirates* (Andrew Nagy); *Empire* (Chris Lupton, Adam Gerrard); *Esquire* (David McKendrick, Declan Fahy, Nick Millington); Simon Esterson; Eyestorm (Angie Davy, Henrik Riis, Carys Lake-Edwards); Garage Museum of Contemporary Art (Brittany Stewart, Kirstine Wallace); *Giant* (Ash Gibson); *Glamour Germany* (Katja Klinger, Nina Meixner); *GQ France* (Paul Chemetov, Marion Tremoy); Grey London (Nils Leonrad); James Grubb; *The Guardian* (Phil Mongredien, Robert L. White, Sarah Habershon, Maggie Murphy, Pauline Doyle, Kate Abbott, Sara Ramsbottom, Sarah Bolesworth, Andrew Stocks, Melanie Carvalho, Katherine Butler, Andrew Mayers, Andrew Tod); *Haaretz* (Nohar Zmora, Yaniv Primak); Human After All (Paul Willoughby); *Internazionale* (Giovanni De Mauro, Pasquale Cavorsi); iShares (Leslie D'Acri, Karen Rossiter, Melinda Kanipe); It's Nice That (Alex Bec, Will Hudson); Jealous Gallery; John Brown Media (Liz Edwards); Leo Burnett / Drug-Free America (Laurie Gustafson, Darren Wright, David Skinner); The London Design Festival (Ben Evans); Lutyens, Prescott & Conran (Peter Prescott); Made Movement (Amy Mainero); *Men's Fitness* (Joe Summa); *Men's Health* (Declan Fahy); Mr Porter (Xanthe Greenhill); Mucho/Cobega (Sonia Herrero); *The New York Times* (Paul Jean, Nicholas Blechman, Alexandra Zsigmond, Jolene Cuyler); *The New Yorker* (Christine Curry); *NME* (Tony Ennis); Ogilvy & Mather, France (Fergus O'Hare, Ginevra Capece, Susan Westre); Outline Editions (Camilla Parsons, Ellie Phillips, Diane Tuckey, Gavin Lucas); Penguin Firsts; Penguin Group (Paul Buckley); Point Five/*Columbia Journalism Review* (Benjamin Levine); Publicis Asia (Jason Pan); *Radio Times* (Julia Noakes); Random House (Suzanne Dean); *Reader's Digest US* (Marti Golon); Scholz & Friends (Stan Gruel); *Scientific American* (Patti Nemoto); Seiden (Eric Houseknecht, Stephen Feinberg, Jill Levy); *Shortlist* (Joanna Moran, Jonathan Pile); G.F. Smith; Sony; *Standpoint* (James Brewster, Ingrid Shields); Studio Blackburn (Paul Blackburn, Susie Blackburn); *The Sunday Times* (Rachel Bailey, Linda Burrows); TBWA\Chiat\Day New York / World Food Programme (Melatan Riden, Jason Souter); *The Telegraph* (Danielle Campbell, David Riley, Gary Cochran); *Time Out London* (Adam Fulrath, Micha Weidmann, Patrick McNamee); *Town/Brave New World* (Lyndsey Price); Trendbüro/*Werte-Index* (Martina Schneider); Victoria and Albert Museum (Nadine Fleischer, Lindsay Pentelow and the team); *De Volkskrant* (Kaj van Ek, Jaap Biemans); *Vrij Nederland* (Guido van Lier); *Wallpaper** (Tony Chambers, Marion Pritchard, Benjamin Kempton, Pei-Ru Keh); *The Washington Post* (Nancy Broadwater); *Washingtonian* (Michael Goesele); White Duck Screen Print; *Wired* (Maren Haupt, Andrew Diprose)

For Dana, Mia and Lili Bar

On the cover: *Evolutionary Thought II*, 2013

First published in the United Kingdom in 2017 by
Thames & Hudson Ltd, 181A High Holborn, London WC1V 7QX

Bittersweet: Noma Bar © 2017 Thames & Hudson Ltd, London
Illustrations by Noma Bar © 2017 Noma Bar
Chineasy images © 2017 Chineasy Ltd
Chapter introductions © 2017 Noma Bar
Foreword © 2017 Michael Bierut

Designed by Studio Fernando Gutiérrez
Texts compiled and edited with Rosie Fairhead

British Library Cataloguing-in-Publication Data
A catalogue record for this book is available from the
British Library

ISBN: 978-0-500-02129-3

Printed and bound in China by C&C Offset Printing Co. Ltd

To find out about all our publications, please visit
www.thamesandhudson.com. There you can subscribe
to our e-newsletter, browse or download our current
catalogue, and buy any titles that are in print.